How To Make Your Ads, Salesletters, And Websites Sell Like Crazy!

Mark Hendricks

SmallBizSuccessCoach.com

Legal Notices: Neither the Author or the Publisher assumes any responsibility for errors, inaccuracies or omissions. Any slights of people or organizations are unintentional. If advice concerning tax, legal or related matters is needed, the services of a qualified professional should be sought. This book is not intended for use as a source of legal, accounting or financial advice. Also some suggestions made in this book concerning sales and marketing and business practices may have inadvertently introduced practices deemed unlawful in certain states or municipalities. You should be aware of the various laws governing advertising, sales, marketing and other business practices in your particular industry and in your marketplace.

The Publisher also notes that certain offers of books, tapes, other products and services have been made in this book and reserves the right to modify or withdraw those offers at any time.

DEDICATION

To all the great sales and marketing pioneers of the past,
present and future who discover, apply and pass
along what really works.

CONTENTS

Special Chapter -- Read This First!

"The Marketing Technology Has Changed... But Human Hopes and Desires Do Not!"

I know how frustrating it is.

You try and try, and just don't seem to get anywhere.

And by anywhere, I mean...

"Make Money!"

You see, I've discovered a few secrets that I'm going to share with you.

And if you're marketing your products or services, whether offline or online, then you'll find this especially worthwhile.

But first, a little background.

We are all bombarded with marketing messages and advertising each day -- by the thousands, whether it be in the newspapers, magazines, TV, radio, postal mail, or by way of the internet, or any other media to get the message to us.

Take the internet, for example...

All you have to do is BROWSE around a little and you'll see so much information that it's hard to sort it all out.

And for MOST computer users, quite frankly, it's...

"Overwhelming!"

They see so many interesting things to BROWSE, that they don't have enough time (or money) to give everything a serious and close look to BUY.

Let me ask you a question to see if what I'm trying to say makes sense to you...

Have you ever walked into a shopping mall store in your city and been greeted by a store employee who asked you...

"May I Help You Find Something?"

...and, of course, the typical automatic response is what?...(you're exactly right)...

"No, I'm Just Browsing."

As shoppers, we've been conditioned to say this over the years, "No, I'm Just Browsing", and so many sales have been lost because of that single question that's asked to the consumer in millions of situations every day, "May I Help You Find Something?"

Now there IS a BIG lesson to learn here from this LITTLE story.

First of all, this consumer in our little store may indeed be, JUST BROWSING and not at all ready to buy! So to assume that the consumer is ready to buy RIGHT NOW (by that I mean, the first time you come in contact with them) is a big mistake.

You see, no matter what STOREFRONT you have (at the mall or electronically online), there are certain very important steps that must be taken when marketing, before your customer is ready to buy.

A few things have to happen...

First, the consumer has to be:

1) ATTRACTED to something that will be of...

2) BENEFIT to the consumer...then enough

3) DESIRE for that BENEFIT must be generated to motivate the consumer to...

4) TAKE ACTION and...

5) BUY.

You see, getting the consumer to buy is what YOU WANT (the store), but the only way to get the consumer to buy...

"Is to give your consumer what HE WANTS FIRST!"

And what does the consumer want?

He or she wants just one of two things (give them both things and it's even better!)

Something that will make him...

1) FEEL GOOD or

2) SOLVE HIS PROBLEM.

In other words, you must...

"Provide a GREAT BIG BENEFIT to the consumer."

So just what was the store employee's (our) big mistake?

We (the store) are concerned...WAY TO SOON...in getting what... WE WANT...instead of letting the consumer get what THEY WANTED...FIRST!

The consumer wasn't even given enough time to have any product or service ATTRACT his or her attention.

Just imagine this scene for a second (it takes place in the mall or at their computer screen!)

Here they are, just walked in and are looking for something to BROWSE at, with no particular thing that they're looking for in mind, and the store employee (we) GOES FOR THE SALE before the customer even has a chance to get COMFORTABLE in the store's (mall or electronic mall) surroundings.

Sometimes it may even take a few visits (or multiple contacts in follow-ups, that's very important...more about that later).

So you say...

"Okay, Okay...but what does this have to do with making your Ads sell like crazy and making more money in your business?"

Here's my point...

Most all of the Ads I see (97% of them at least) are making these very same kinds of mistakes over and over again. And I've discovered a little secret I'm going to share with you.

"You've got to let your prospective customers BROWSE just a little, just like in the neighborhood mall, before you ask them to buy."

This is very important...please don't miss the point I'm making...

You've got to let them go through all of these same steps... "step...by...step...by...step."

First by being ATTRACTED to your information, then by letting them find out for themselves what BENEFITS you are offering them, and letting their WANTS and DESIRES build up slowly to the PURCHASE of your offer. And sometimes it takes a few visits with you (or repetitions of your ad/offer) before they're ready to buy.

There are secret strategies that have been used by direct response marketers for over a hundred years that most modern marketers just don't know about. And the big-shot Madison Avenue advertisers have abandoned them because they seem to be "too simple" for today's so-called... Sophisticated Shoppers.

"What a big mistake!"

And what most businesses don't understand is that what has worked in the past to get response from consumers will work today if applied properly on the new technology of the Net.

"The Marketing Technology Has Changed... But Human Hopes and Desires Do Not!"

These basic ideas are so important that I've got to repeat them one more time...

Using these little known secret techniques is the way to get your Browser's attention so that they'll be ATTRACTED to your ad (first), then they'll be given the chance to develop a DESIRE for your product/service by seeing the BENEFITS to them that will lead them into WANTING your product/service enough for them to TAKE ACTION and BUY.

Which is exactly what YOU WANT, isn't it?

"WARNING: Don't Take This Introduction Section Lightly!

It contains the groundwork basics that we'll expand on in the rest of the book!"

"Be Sure To Return To This Section...And Read It Over And Over Again!"

Remember...the basics are what always works.

Okay, let's turn the page and get started...

(go on to the next chapter now)

Chapter One...

"The Absolutely Biggest #1 Mistake That Most People Make When Marketing...And How To Avoid It, Once And For All!"

Since you've probably been online a while now, and have gotten pretty used to using Email, you've most likely made this observation already, but I'll ask you anyway...

Have you noticed that most folks write short and bare-bones Email messages?

I mean they write messages as if a simple-minded computer who only understands binary language was at the other end of the modem line, instead of...

"a real, live, and breathing human being."

Think about it.

You, a real, live, and breathing human, are trying to communicate your ideas to someone hundreds or thousands of miles away through this maze of high technology.

You're trying to motivate them to buy your product or services, and develop a profitable long-term business relationship (more about that in a later chapter).

And just when you're really about to say something that really hits home with your prospective customer, you all of a sudden remember that you're at a computer keyboard and darned if you don't completely remove all of your God-given natural skills to communicate to another real, live, and breathing human, and start to type out these short, to the point, translated into "computer-ese" messages, that are absolutely (oh, I can't stand it anymore)...

"Proper "Net"-iquette."

In other words...

"Stripped Bare Of Any Real Live Human Emotion!"

My online marketing friend, please don't make this mistake.

Just because we have all this terrific technology in front of us, and we're plugged in all over the world so that we can communicate to anyone who's on the other end (It is amazing, isn't it? I pinch myself to see if I'm dreaming, and I still can't believe it, can you?), it doesn't mean that you have to homogenize your words just for the behalf of the technology.

So how do you "humanize" your sales messages?

"You've Got To Learn To Write Like You Talk"

Can you remember back to junior high English class? (I know it's painful, but bear with me.)

They taught us all "the rules" of proper grammar.

No dangling participles.

No ending with a prepositional phrase.

They taught you how to write "textbook perfect".

And do you remember what most of the textbooks have in common?

That's right!

Most "textbook-perfect-written" textbooks have one major problem...

"They're Boring!"

You, my marketing friend, do not have this luxury!

You don't have the "Miss Primproper" authority to force your online target prospect to continue reading your sales letters.

If you aren't interesting, entertaining, and most of all, benefiting your reader with each and every phrase and from their point of view, they will stop reading and you've lost your opportunity to gain a customer.

"You can't be boring, not for even one second."

If you are, then zap (or crumple if they printed out your letter), you're gone...and they're off thinking about something else.

So what's my best advice?

Learn to write like you talk.

Have a conversation with your reader/customer, by way of the printed word...just like you're there with them.

Don't think of yourself just typing letters and words into your word processor to download onto somebody.

Think of how you would say things if you and they were sitting in easy chairs, talking about the good ol' days like old friends.

One to one.

Heart to heart.

Be a real person.

Talk plain and down to earth.

No hi-tech psycho-babble that takes a rocket scientist to figure out with a slide rule what you're saying.

Just use a simple...personal...conversational tone in everything that you write and you'll do tons better.

Here's a few tips:

Tip #1 --- If you're having trouble forgetting what "Miss Primproper" taught you in junior high English class, just pull out a little cheapo cassette recorder and record a conversation of you and a friend/spouse discussing your topic and offer.

Don't edit yourself while you talk things over.

Just talk freely.

Let the other person ask questions during the conversation...just like they normally would, right?

And you answer them.

"Now you've really got something."

You've got a real-live conversation between two real-live breathing people recorded on tape that can be transcribed and edited.

Don't edit it up too much.

Just take out the "uuuhs and uuums" and re-order things a little so your best beneficial points are made early on.

Tip #2 --- Have you noticed how I'm using paragraphs that rarely have more than three sentences in them?

And many times, only one sentence?

Like this one.

Believe me, "Miss Primproper" would not approve!

"But dear Miss Primproper never made tens of thousands of dollars (or more) from writing a sales letter, now did she?"

By using paragraphs that have only three, two, or one sentences, you give your reader...

"variety and the look of something that's easy to read."

You've got to make things EASY for your reader.

Most of us have too many distractions already going on in our lives. And you're here to make things easy for your customer.

That's why they will give you their money.

Because...remember?

You're giving them...

"Good Feelings And Solutions To Their Problems...Easy Solutions!"

I know, I know, I said this before already. Look there's no rule that says you can't say things twice or even three times to make your point.

Tip #3 --- As a matter of fact, you should practice getting very good at saying the same thing five different ways.

Why, you ask? (by the way...see how you just asked a question in our conversation here?)

It's because everyone learns and understands things from a different perspective, and it's your job to communicate to your consumer in the way that they can understand it the easiest. Not the way that it's easiest for you to understand.

And since you're having this one-to-one conversation with someone who is not physically there to ask you questions to clear things up as you go, doesn't it make sense to explain your point in a few different ways to help them grasp the idea?

Here's a few lead-in lines that you can use for stating different approaches for the same topic:

By that I mean... -- Stated another way...

Or you could say... -- Another way to look at it is...

Tip #4 --- Use different layout techniques to make the page more interesting to look at, and easier to read.

I'm sure you've noticed that I not only use different length sentences and paragraphs, but I've also put the major points of our discussion in...

"bold headings set in different type-set."

Now just for a second, flip back through the first few pages of this book and see how easy it is to skim for the important points.

And notice how you'll find things quickly that interest you and you start reading the details between the bold headings. You see, we read at two different levels at different times, and some people lean one way or the other in their natural reading style.

"Some People Are Skimmers And Some People Are Detailers"

And since you don't know what kind of reader you've got, and you don't know how much time they have to read your letter, you give them both ways to read your letter.

The "Detailer" who has some time now will read the details between the bold section heads that catch his attention, and the "Skimmer" who is short on time will be able to skim the bold section heads and then come back later to read the details of your offer.

Tip #5 --- Now here's an important point...

In your online letters, you can't get quite as fancy as with your laser-printed layouts. But you can use (I'm switching now to the most common used type-style online):

1) Capital Letters For Each Word

2) ALL CAPITAL LETTERS FOR A REAL IMPORTANT POINT --- USE SPARINGLY!

3) "Use quotes around statements. It makes them more important."

4) Use various special symbols to make your letter appealing to the eye, such as:

=== Your Message Here ===

$$$ Your Message Here $$$

/\/\/\ Your Message Here /\/\/\

======================

>> Your Message Here <<<

======================

5) Use short paragraphs and even one sentence paragraphs.

6) Use "thought connectors"...like those little dots that I just put in this line.

7) Put things in parentheses (to make your side comments).

8) "Of course, you could MIX AND MATCH some of these techniques...to give a Special Look to a certain section of your letter (this would be used only for special emphasis only)."

9) You can use lists, like I have done here.

10) The point is to make your letter visually inviting to read, easy to read, and for gracious sakes, whatever you do...

"Don't Be Boring!"

Tip #6 --- You've probably noticed, or maybe you haven't, that I'm not afraid to use contractions. That's those words that are really two words but you drop a letter and put in the (') symbol. Example:

you've --- for "you have"

haven't --- for "have not"

I'm --- for "I am"

that's --- for "that is"

Why do I do this?

It's because that's how we talk in real life.

And that's what you want to do when you write a sales letter to your target consumer.

Tip #7 --- So feel free to drive "Miss Primproper" absolutely nuts with your dangling participles, endless use of prepositional phase endings, one sentence paragraphs, and contractions in written form.

It'll give you great satisfaction to write her a nice thank you note (now be nice, use proper grammar with complete sentence structure) letting her know the success you've had by knowing the proper grammar and writing rules (but not necessarily using them!).

Please, always remember, to get your message straight to the heart of your reader...

"Write Like You Talk!"

P.S. Or if Miss Primproper had her way, "You must learn to write as if you are speaking."

P.P.S. Which one do you think gets the message across better?

(go on to the next chapter now)

Chapter Two...

"How To Find The People Who Will Buy Whatever You Want To Sell Them!"

One of the first questions you should be asking yourself is just exactly...

"Who is your market?

In other words, just exactly who is going to buy what you're offering?

If you say, "Everybody." Then we're in BIG trouble.

If your market is everybody, then your real market is nobody.

Probably the easiest way to describe what I mean is to compare it to fishing.

The absolutely easiest way to catch fish is to put your bait in a barrel that contains...

"a whole bunch of hungry fish."

Now I know that sounds like an over-simplification, but it's the truth, isn't it?

They're all grouped together. They're hungry. You've got the right food. You drop bait in. They bite.

Here's a little three step secret to the successful marketing of anything!

"You've got to...

reach the right market...
with the right message...
at the right time."

Simple as that.

Think about it for a second.

Let's use our fishing example.

The right market - you've found them...they're in the barrel!

The right message - fat and juicy wiggling worms.

The right time - they are hungry...now!

Do you think they're going to bite?

Yes!

Now let's see for a second what happens if you're missing just one piece of our 3-step secret.

Scenario #1:

You go fishing in your bathtub (wrong market)

Fat and juicy wiggling worms.

They are hungry...now.

Doesn't work, does it? Why? There's no fish where you put the bait.

Sure, there's hungry fish out there, right now, but you put your bait in your bathtub instead of the barrel.

Scenario #2:

You go fishing in a barrel...you found them.

You bait your hook with brussel sprouts (instead of fat and juicy wiggling worms).

They are hungry...now.

No bites. How come? Wrong bait.

Scenario #3:

You go fishing in a barrel...you found them.

You bait your hook with fat and juicy wiggling worms.

They are NOT hungry now.

No bites. You guessed it, wrong timing.

Okay, okay. You get the point. But that's the quickest and easiest way to describe exactly what has to happen when you're marketing your product or service.

And we'll be discussing ways to deal with each of these three steps in the process.

But remember...

"Right Market...Right Message... Right Time."

Okay, let's get started with finding the right market.

Most people make one gigantic error when deciding how to go about selling their products/services.

They decide, first, the product/service that they want to offer, and then try and offer it to the market.

This is a very expensive and frustrating mistake.

Let me share a little secret that is literally worth a pile or three of money to you.

Make things easy for yourself and...

"Find the Market First!"

That's right, before you decide what product/service to offer...

"Find A Group Of Fish...Who Have Shown That They Like To Eat The Same Bait... And Who Are Hungry Now! And Then, (Now Don't Argue With Me On This One)...

Give Them That Bait!"

You've got to give people what THEY want...not what YOU THINK they should want.

If you can give people what they really want, then you'll "catch a lotta fish!"

Okay, good, you've hung in there this long with me, now let's see how we can apply this "masters of direct marketing secret" to marketing online.

Here's the problem...

Where is the market and what do they want?

Now put on your thinking cap and follow along.

Fish like to swim in schools. Sheep like to be in a flock. Cattle like to be in a herd.

Important Point...

"People Like To Belong To Groups So They Can Associate and Feel Comfortable and Be With Like-Minded People."

Have you ever heard of the "group mentality"? Or "herd mentality"?

Sure you have.

Now you may want to argue with me and say, "Well, what about independent thinkers?"

May I suggest that "independent thinkers" love to discuss the benefits of "independent thinking" with other "independent thinkers". So they really do function in groups, don't they?

I'll explain why people like to be in groups in a later chapter. It's actually a fact of our own biology.

Anyway, I digress.

Now where do you figure we could find people who are "flocking" together in "groups" like a "school of fish"?

Right you are.

Subscribers to newspapers, to certain magazines (whether special interest or business industry), they receive newsletters by mail or internet, they belong to clubs and organizations, and all the other niche areas where people group together.

Let's talk about little ads in the back of a magazine first (this will also apply to the other areas).

You've probably noticed that the ads are divided up into sections, or areas of interest.

And do you know who goes looking in those sections.

Actually it's a few kind of folks.

People who are looking to buy (remember to feel better or solve a problem).

People who are looking to sell (marketing their product/service --- your competition by the way).

And those who are just "lurking" (browsers, window-shoppers, sort of like fish who are swimming in the stream, but not hungry enough at the moment to bite).

Now remember...right market, right message, right time.

The first thing you need to do is to go browsing a little just to look around this "pond" we call the magazine.

One thing is immediately seen...there are a lot of messages posted there (or bait being cast).

But that doesn't mean that the "fish" are biting, does it?

No. It just means that there are a lot of people "fishing".

Now let me ask you a question. If you saw a fisherman come back to the same lake and use the same bait over and over again (expending time, energy, and money), do you think that you could say one of a few things about him?

#1) he's not catching anything and he's just likes to "go" fishing.

#2) he's not catching anything and he's just plain wasting his time and money.

#3) he's catching fish.

So the quickest and least expensive way for you to look for...

"...the right market and the right message..."

…is to look at others who are consistently there. Because they're either successful, dumb, or just there for the "entertainment value".

You're looking for the successful ones.

Look at their ads, and sales letters. Get on their lists, and study what they're doing.

And come up with a product/service (the message) that you can provide to that same "school of fish" (the right market). Interestingly, it doesn't have to be a new product/service. It could be just a slight improvement or variation on what they already bought.

"If the fish likes worms, chances are the fish will like more worms tomorrow, when he's hungry again."

So now you've found the fish, you found the bait, now you've just got to find out when they're hungry.

Now just like in fishing, you've got to be patient.

Let's say that you've found the pond with fish in it (the market).

And you've put the right kind of bait out from watching the successful fisherman (the message).

And they're nibbling, but not biting, hook, line and sinker.

In other words, they're sort of just browsing or window-shopping.

My marketing friend, that happens a lot in fishing...and marketing too.

They may nibble (request for your information), but just aren't hungry enough yet to bite (buy).

So what do I suggest you do?

Send it to them again in a few weeks, and then again in a few more weeks.

At least three times (seven or more contacts would be great).

Why, you ask?

Number one, they did say they were interested.

And by not buying on the first try, they didn't say they weren't interested. They just didn't respond.

Why didn't they respond, who knows?

Why don't you respond to offers?

Didn't receive it...couldn't print it out...didn't have time to read it...didn't have time to think about it...didn't have the money right then...had to cook dinner...the phone rang...put in a pile of paper on your desk to read later...lost it...and on and on and on.

See my point?

Sure, the offer is REAL IMPORTANT to you, the seller, You want them to buy now, don't you?

But the buyer has got a bazillion other things going on in their life and all they did was sort of "raise their hand" a little and said "I'm interested" enough to ask for you to send your information to them.

They didn't even promise to read any of it, did they?

No, they just asked for information.

Now having somebody take the action to ask for information sure beats the pants off of just sending your whole offer out blindly to the masses (remember, if everybody is your market, then nobody is).

So with all this other stuff going on in their lives, there's a real good chance that your offer...

"Just Didn't Make It To The Front Burner!"

They may have your info sitting on their desk someplace, it may be stored as a file on their hard drive.

You don't know.

The thing that you DO know is that at least they asked for the information. So yes they have identified themselves as a "fish", who does nibble at bait, but for the time being, may not be hungry.

So what do you do?

This may shock you (and I am repeating myself to make this very point)...send it to them again.

Maybe with a reminder that they asked for this a few weeks ago, and you thought they might have misplaced it or lost it in the shuffle.

Or you may have to "jiggle your bait" a little (try a new headline, test a different price, state stronger benefits, give them more information so they can decide, package together some other products/services to add-on to your main offer, try a stronger and/or longer guarantee, etc.).

That's just part of the process.

That's what makes some people good fishermen (marketers) and others not.

Always remember to...

"Reach The Right Market...
With The Right Message...
At The Right Time."

Here's another way to find out more about your market...

Go online and browse around the posting boards on websites, newsgroups, discussion groups, and forums.

You'll find people asking for help with their problems. And you can even make a list of those people who have left messages asking for information.

Are they a hungry fish, or what?

You'll also find files called "FAQ". Meaning "Frequently Asked Questions".

And my "Marketing Maniac", I'm here to tell you that...

"It's a goldmine to you!"

It's like getting the fish you are fishing for to tell you exactly what "bait to use, when they're hungry, and what barrel to find them in."

WARNING: If you plan to market your services online -- You Can Not Blatantly Advertise Your Product/Service In These Newsgroups, Discussion Groups, Or Forums. You may get VERY NASTY mail and have your Email box jam-packed, costing you a lot of time and money, and what's worse you could be banned from your online service.

And...do not send unsolicited email to people online. The same things I just mentioned may happen.

More about how to solve that problem later, you can get people to request your email.

Now let's talk about the most important asset that you will ever have as a marketer online.

"It's The List."

In other, your special list of people who have said they are interested in feeling better, solving a problem, or both, and have expressed an interest by taking action to ask for information and/or have bought from you.

Actually, we just described two lists, didn't we?

People who said they may buy...and people who are buyers.

Which do you think is most valuable?

Let that question sit for a few chapters. We'll talk about it later.

But for now let's talk about...

"How To Develop Your Own Hot Lead List."

Very simply, use what's called a "2-step" ad.

Put a teaser ad (one that arouses curiosity) in the magazine, newspaper, postcard, classifieds, or attach it at the end of your contribution to an onlinne newsgroup/forum (not blatant), that will get the reader to look at your message and respond to receive a "Special Report" or more information.

Let's say that you found a classified section for fly fisherman, and you've come up with a new, "sure-to-get-fish-on-the-hook" fly.

So in your little ad you write...

FREE REPORT Reveals New Proven Fly Fishing Secret

They read your ad and they not a long explanation, and not your offer immediately thrust upon them, but instead they see a little more information and an offer to send them a "Special Report" or more information if they just contact you requesting "Fly Fishing Secret".

Sort of like this ...

FREE REPORT Reveals New Proven Fly Fishing Secret

Dear Friend:

A new free report is now available that will show the new and proven secret to successful fly fishing. To get your copy of this Free Report, all you have to do is [call, visit, write, email] and ask for the Fly Fishing Secret.

Phil Phisher
www.flyfish.com
Voice: 987-555-1234
Fax: 987-555-9876

P.S. You'll wonder why nobody ever thought of this before.

There now, see how simple it can be.

So then what, you send out your full length letter and offer and more importantly for the long term...

"You now have their name on your list!"

And that is really what you are after first. Just get them to "raise their hand" llittle to let you know they are interested.

It's your first job to develop a list of people who are interested in what you have to offer.

Remember earlier when I said that if everyone is your market, then no one is your market.

This is what I'm talking about here.

All you want to do with your initial little ad is to find people who have enough self-motivation to take action and respond to your ad.

A couple of thoughts about the little ad sample above.

You notice that Phil Phisher used his REAL NAME to "sign" the letter with.

That's because you're trying to start a "real, live, and breathing" human being relationship through the technology that is in the way.

And did you notice that Phil Phisher gave the reader his phone number and fax number too.

I find that people are very wary of each other these days.

And you know what, they absolutely should be.

And as an honest and reputable marketer you should take the first step in humanizing your relationship to your customers.

And this is one way to do it.

Show them that you're accessible and you welcome one-on-one communication by way of Email, voice, fax, carrier pigeon...whatever it takes.

Now you could use another technique to qualify your prospects even further.

It's called a 3-step ad.

Basically it's the same beginning as the 2-step ad.

First step...a small ad that gets their attention and asks them to respond to get more information.

Second step...use a recorded telephone message that discusses the topic, gives them more info, discusses the problem and what happens if they don't solve their problem, emphasizes the benefits and creates more desire and curiosity, and asks them to respond AGAIN for very detailed information about your offer.

Now by doing the first and second step prior to sending them the full length sales letter you have assured yourself that...

"This Fish Is Really Hungry."

And then third, you send them the full sales letter (the juiciest bait) for them to really pour over and bite into.

By using three steps you will eliminate most all of the "nibblers, tire-kickers, time-wasters", and people who really aren't going to take action.

But in all things...test, test, test.

You could also write news releases and articles targeted to your markets special interests and have that info published in their newsletters, magazines, and newspapers they read, etc.

Begin by writing interesting short letters and news releases. Remember interesting, alive and breathing human...and not boring!

Here's the trick. Don't tell them all that you know. And don't tell them how to solve their problem. Let them know the big benefits and great feelings they'll have when their problem is solved. And just give them enough hints so they'll want to get another layer of detailed knowledge.

And at the end of your short letter, include your name, Email address, voice, fax, pigeon's name, etc....

And in the P.S. let them know that if they would like further information that you have made available a free special report called "Fly Fishing Secrets" that is now available that will show the new and proven secret to successful fly fishing. To get your copy of this Free Report, all you have to do is [call, visit, write, email] and ask for the Fly Fishing Secret.

And guess what, you've just got their name on your HOT LIST and now you begin your 2-step or 3-step series, and follow-up steps to convert them to your customer.

And always remember, don't just send them one letter.

Send them multiple letters (at least three, maybe more) spread out 3-4 weeks apart will do nicely. Most marketers give up to soon. Studies have shown that it takes 7 contacts with your prospect before you really have developed a position in their mind.

And your Ads are one step, the sales letter is the second (and possibly third), so you can see it's gonna take a few more tosses of the bait before most people are going to bite and buy what you're offering them.

So let's wrap this up.

Here's the little three step secret to successfully marketing anything!

"You've got to...

reach the right market...
with the right message...
at the right time."

Simple as that.

(go on to the next chapter now)

Chapter Three...

"How To Write Ad Headlines That Get Your Offer Seen By The Thousands!"

Okay, let's get going on the very first thing your prospect sees once you have found them through research where your prospect "hangs out" or looks for things that interest them.

The very first thing that your prospect is going to see that will start the whole process going is what's called your headline.

Now let's talk just a second about headlines.

Think about your local newspaper.

When you pick it up to read in the morning what is it that you're looking at as you quickly BROWSE the front page?

"That's Right...The Headlines."

The headlines grab your attention, and in a glance of a second, either peak your curiosity to read the article, or you skim ahead to the next headline.

Interesting, isn't it?

All of those articles that are read (or aren't read), all because of their headlines.

"My friend, the headline is the single most important part of your marketing success."

Before your prospect ever gets to hear your benefits, get to know you, hear your offer, they must first see and be attracted to your ad.

So you could say that...

"Your Headline Is Your Ad...For Your Ad!"

As a matter of fact, you would be very accurate if you say that 80% (or more) of the success of any offer or ad is the headline. So be very sure to spend lots of time trying and testing different headlines.

Here's something that'll be sure to keep you motivated...

"You're Only One Headline Away From Riches!"

Let me give you just one more idea to think about. One little secret that can make your Ads more effective...IMMEDIATELY!

The Ads online tend to be written from the seller's point of view, instead of the buyer's point of view.

This my Online Friend is a big, big mistake.

And believe me when I tell you, the only point of view that counts is...

"The Customer's Point Of View."

So the first thing to do is to make your headline of GREAT BENEFIT to your targeted BROWSER, so that AT LEAST they will be attracted to what your Ad is all about.

"Remember...think of your HEADLINE as an AD for your AD."

You may have to come up with a bunch of headlines and test them, one against the other to find the one that does the best your particular product/service and offer.

Then, make sure in your information section, that you quickly state the GREATEST BENEFIT from the CONSUMER'S POINT OF VIEW that you can make. This will help things get started on the right foot.

I can't emphasize too much the importance of HEADLINES. By testing one versus another, it's been found that one headline will outpull another by OVER 1700%!!

"That's right...OVER 1700% !!"

And that's with the SAME information in the body of the ad!

Here's a little quiz for you, just to show you how a change in headline can make a tremendous difference in the results of your marketing.

Now remember, the body of the sales message was the same for each of these sets of headlines.

I'll give you the answers after you've tried to say which headline got the most response.

By the way, these headlines are found in a classic book by John Caples called "How To Make Your Advertising Make Money" -- get it.

Okay, here we go with the first pair...

Set #1

If you are a careful driver you can save money on car insurance.

How to turn your careful driving into money.

Set #2

How to make your food taste better.

How to get your cooking bragged about.

Set #3

How to do your Christmas shopping in 5 minutes.

The gift that comes 12 times a year.

Set #4

How to get a loan of $500.

When should a family get a loan.

Set #5

Announcing an important revision of the Bible.

Most important Bible news in 340 years.

Okay, did you pick your winners?

(Go ahead, I'll wait.)

Now before you see the winner from each pair, understand this very important point...

"You Do Not Have The Right To Tell Your Market What They Will Respond To. If You Will Just Listen, By Way Of Their Response (or lack of response), You Will Know What Headline To Use After Testing A Few Different Ones."

Alright, let's look at the results and be amazed...

The Winners Are...

Set #1

If You Are A Careful Driver You Can Save Money On Car Insurance
(this headline pulled 50% more leads than the other)

Set #2

How To Get Your Cooking Bragged About
(this headline brought 42% more requests than the other)

Set #3

How To Do Your Christmas Shopping In 5 Minutes
(this headline brought 90% more sales than the other)

Set #4

How To Get A Loan Of $500
(this headline pulled more than 100% better than the other)

Set #5

Most Important Bible News In 340 Years
(this headline sold 71% more Bibles than the other)

Now the first question that may come to your mind is...WHY?

Unfortunately, in marketing, that's not a good question.

And believe me, if you will just listen to your marketplace, they WILL tell you very loudly with their response (orders for your product/service) or with their silence.

You'll go nuts and broke trying to figure out WHY people do what they do.

(A little note: I'll talk about why people do things in an upcoming chapter, but one thing for sure, people DON'T do things for purely logical reasons.

So don't go nuts trying to figure out LOGICALLY WHY people do what they do or don't do, just accept it and move ahead.)

You see, by presenting a few headlines to your market (your prospects), you're letting them choose what they have an interest in.

Now let's do a little experiment, remember Phil Phisher, our fly fishing expert?

How could "ol' flyfishin' Phil" use these five headlines as a beginning point for his "Fly Fishing Secrets" ad and report?

Okay, let's look at each headline separately...

If You Are A Careful Driver You Can Save Money On Car Insurance

How about for Phil...

If You Are Frustrated Fly Fisherman You Can Now Catch More Fish In An Hour Than You Do All Weekend

Here's another...

How To Get Your Cooking Bragged About

For Phil...

How To Get Your Flyfishing Bragged About

And another...

How To Do Your Christmas Shopping In 5 Minutes

Phil's version...

How To Tie "Record-Catch" Flies In 5 Minutes

Here's one more...

How To Get A Loan Of $500

How about this for Phil...

How To Get A 7-Day Fly Fisherman's Dream Vacation For $500

And finally...

Most Important Bible News In 340 Years

And for Phil...

Most Important Fly Fishing News In 50 Years

Do you see how you can take other people's successful headlines and use them as springboards for your own headlines?

Don't reinvent the wheel.

Get ideas from winners and modify them to fit your situation.

Okay, now here's a way to jump-start your brain when coming up with headlines for your ads.

I call it...

"The Headline Template."

These are some of the most successful headlines of all times. Go through the whole list with your product/service in mind and "fill in the blanks" where I've indicated by CAPITALIZING certain words, just like we did for Phil Phisher and his Fly Fishing Secrets.

1. They Laughed When I SAT DOWN AT THE PIANO --- But When I Started To PLAY!

2. Do You Make These Mistakes In ENGLISH?

3. How A STRANGE ACCIDENT Saved Me From BALDNESS

4. Who Else Wants A SCREEN STAR FIGURE?

5. Announcing The New FORD CARS For 1994 (change year also)

6. Are You Ashamed Of The SMELLS IN YOUR HOME?

7. Buy No DESK Until You've Seen The SENSATION OF THE BUSINESS SHOW

8. Can You Talk About BOOKS With The Rest Of Them?

9. CAR INSURANCE At Low Cost --- If You're A CAREFUL DRIVER

10. CAR Owners ... Save ONE GALLON OF GAS In Every TEN

11. Double Your Money Back If This Isn't The Best ONION SOUP You Ever TASTED

12. Free Book Tells You TWELVE Secrets Of BETTER LAWN CARE

13. Get Rid Of MONEY Worries For Good

14. GIRLS...Want Quick CURLS?

15. Greatest BIBLE News In 341 Years (change number of years too)

16. 10 Ways To Beat The HIGH COST OF LIVING

17. How To Stop WORRYING

18. How The Next NINETY Days Can Change Your LIFE

19. The Secret Of MAKING PEOPLE LIKE YOU

20. PLAY GUITAR In 7 Days Or Money Back

21. To MEN Who Want To QUIT WORK SOME DAY

Here, as a little bonus for you, are the...

"Top 10 Words Used In The 100 Most Successful Headlines Of All Time."

you 31 --- your 14 --- how 12 --- new 10 --- who 8

money 6 --- now 4 --- people 4 --- want 4 --- why 4

Did you notice the frequency of each word in those 100 headlines?

Did you see that YOU or YOUR appeared in 45 out of a 100 great money-making headlines?

Remember how I said you must present the information in the Customer's Point of View?

The best way to do that is to...

"Use the words YOU and YOUR as much as possible."

Always try to get YOU into your headlines and the body of your letter (copy).

It's also great to get the word NEW into your messages. People are always wanting something NEW, aren't they? Have you ever heard someone ask you, "What's New?"

Lots of times, right?

People want to know what's NEW. You've probably heard that, "Inquiring minds want to know!"

And then there's the all time favorite...HOW.

People want to know HOW TO SOLVE PROBLEMS...HOW TO MAKE MONEY...HOW TO SAVE TIME...HOW TO LOSE WEIGHT...HOW TO WIN FRIENDS...HOW TO DO THIS AND HOW TO DO THAT.

Soooo, next time you're coming up with headlines try and get YOU...NEW...and HOW TO in there.

They've worked forever and they'll work for YOU in the future.

Remember what I said earlier...

"The Marketing Technology Has Changed... But Human Hopes and Desires Do Not!"

Okay, you want more, how about...

"The 21 Magic Words That Can Make You Rich!"

suddenly --- miracle --- now --- magic --- announcing --- offer

introducing --- quick --- improvement --- easy --- amazing

wanted --- sensational --- challenge --- remarkable --- compare

revolutionary --- bargain --- startling --- hurry

And last, but certainly not least (and probably more effective than any other motivating word that we know of)...

"FREE!"

Use FREE every chance you get!

In this chapter are the beginnings of your success. Read it over and over again. Come back to this chapter every time you're brainstorming for headlines ideas. Use the "headline template" to help you get started.

Come up with your own "hot headlines" that you see every day in your Email and postal mail. Those direct marketers are spending tens of thousands and millions of dollars to send out those so called "junk-mail" pieces to you. Do you really think they would mail all that stuff out if it wasn't making them a fortune?

Start making a "scrapbook" of great headlines that you see and make them into your own money-making headlines.

Remember...

"You're Only One Headline Away From Riches!"

(go on to the next chapter now)

Chapter Four...

"The Secret Seven-Step Process That You Must Use To Make Your Offer Irresistible!"

Now you've gotten your prospect to ask for more information about your product/service by sending an Email message back to you after seeing your classified ad posting, or reading your short and helpful message letter in the newsgroup/forum discussion.

Terrific!

Congratulations!

You've been successful at the first step in our two (or three or more) step process.

Now you've got to send them a Special Report (disguised as a sales letter) that expands on the benefits that you put in your headline and the body of the copy in your posting.

In this chapter I'm going to talk about the classic 4-step "AIDA" formula for writing and expand on it, and then give you the secret seven-step process that you must use to make your offer irresistible.

But first, let me stress a very important point.

In all of your communication with your prospects and customers, you should know that when writing headlines, sales letters, Email, follow-ups, you name it --- your writing is basically nothing more than...

"Salesmanship In Print."

The concepts and steps are the same whether you're talking one-on-one, face-to-face, to a prospect/customer or sending out a Email ad or sales letter to thousands online.

Always remember to write like you talk, and write your sales letters with a personal and conversational tone. Just like you're sitting down face-to-face with the reader.

Here's the classic formula for writing any sales letter. It's called the "AIDA" formula.

1. ATTENTION - you've got to get your reader's attention

2. INTEREST - you must develop the reader's interest

3. DESIRE - you've got to build the reader's desire

4. ACTION - and finally, you must motivate your reader to action.

If you did nothing more than used this AIDA formula as an outline for your sales messages, you would be way ahead of the game. It will help organize your thoughts and keep you on track in communicating and motivating your reader, in the proper steps and sequence that your reader must travel to respond to your offer.

Now let's expand upon this just a little bit to get a little more thread of continuity:

First, the consumer has to be:

1) ATTRACTED to something that will be of...

2) BENEFIT to the consumer...then enough

3) DESIRE for that BENEFIT must be generated to motivate the consumer to...

4) TAKE ACTION and...

5) BUY.

Do you see how simple and logical the progression is?

Each step naturally flows into the next seamlessly.

Just like a conversation.

Just like talking.

But let's get even more specific. Let me give you the step-by-step, play-by-play method I call...

"The Secret Seven-Step Process That You Must Use To Make Your Sales Offer Irresistible."

Let's begin with...

Step #1 - You must say something that will get your reader's attention.

This is your headline.

The single purpose of your headline is to attract your reader's attention and to get them to read the body of your ad or sales letter.

Your headline should specifically target the prospect that you want and get them to react by moving ahead to the next step in the process, which is reading the body copy.

As we've said before, think of your headline as an ad for your ad.

Always state your biggest benefit or give a big promise in your ad that states clearly to the right prospect exactly what solution, to what problem, you are offering.

Always come up with at least 10 (or more) headlines, and then test them one against the other to see which one pulls the best response. After you've written all of these headlines, you can even combine them into more headlines, or use some as sub headlines too.

Step #2 - You must tell your reader exactly why they should be interested in what you have to offer.

Now you're going to talk to your reader about the specific benefits that you are offering.

Please, please, please...never assume that your reader fully understands all the benefits that you are offering. It's your responsibility to spell out the benefits one-by-one to your reader.

There is a tendency to want to just begin listing the features of your product/service.

This is the sure way to bore your reader. By only listing the features, you're not giving the reader the benefits of your offer.

Important point...

"People Only Buy Benefits...Not Features."

Step #3 - You must tell them why they should care about your message.

This is your chance to answer the three questions that always comes to the mind of your prospect, namely:

1. So what?

2. Who cares?

3. What's In It For Me? --- they are only receiving on radio station "WII-FM"

Anytime you communicate with a prospect/customer they will be asking themselves these three questions before considering doing business with you..

Any statement that you make about your product/service is being analyzed in their mind with these three questions and it's YOUR responsibility to answer these questions for the prospect/customer --- don't allow them to interpret for themselves...they may come up with the wrong answer!

That's why they're having the problems they're having, right?

How do you answer these questions?

By writing into your copy a little story about others who had the same hopes, fears, and dreams. And how by following your recommendations they received the benefits of solving their problems and are now happier or more successful.

Step #4 - You must prove that what you're saying is true.

Use specific examples of how your product/service has helped others.

Use specific numbers that quantify results that have been achieved.

Use testimonials and/or endorsements from people who have gotten the benefits of your product/service.

Use quotes from the media and other experts on the topic.

Use anything you can to provide them with a preponderance of proof that what you are saying is true and beneficial for them.

Step #5 - You must list all the benefits of your product/service.

Now is the time where you can list all of the benefits that your customer will get from the features of your product/service. But don't just start listing the features of your product/service.

I mean heart surgeons don't start telling people about how they've got the sharpest and shiniest scalpels, now do they?

Of course not.

They are giving the patient hope that if the procedure is successful they may being able to live for another 5...10...20 years --- instead of dying tomorrow.

Here's a simple formula...

You'll get <list benefit> from <feature>.

A brief classic example:

You get perfectly round 1/4" holes from this tungsten steel 1/4" drill bit.

(1/4" holes is the desired benefit...the tungsten steel is a feature of the 1/4" drill bit)

You see how you've spoken to the customers interest first.

Now once you've done a good job of telling them about all the benefits they'll receive from your product/service and answering all of their questions to the satisfaction of your prospect/customer, something very interesting usually happens --- in their mind or sometimes they will ask you verbally...

"What's In It For You?"

You see, once they see how your product/service benefits them, all of a sudden they sense that there may be a catch or something.

This is what happens when you've been very successful at showing the prospect/customer the benefits that they will receive from your product/service --- by the way, if you've only talked about the features of your product/service, they are still hung up on questions 1-2-3 (so what..who cares...what's in it for me?) listed above and you'll need to do a better job describing the benefits that those features provide your customer.

So how do you answer the question, "What in it for you?"

Very simply restate a few of the most important benefits to the prospect/customer and then tell them the truth --- that by providing these beneficial products/services to them you receive (fill in the blank).

No fancy answer usually needed. Just plain talk.

Step #6 - You must tell the reader how to order.

Don't make them figure out for themselves how to order.

Make it easy for them.

Give them your best money-back guarantee.

Do everything you possibly can to help them along at this point to write you a check, give you a call with their credit, fax in their order, Email their info, etc.

Provide them with the order form.

Say "Here's what you do now."

And then tell them...step-by-step-by-step.

Step #7 - You must ask them to order right away.

If given the chance people will procrastinate. So you must encourage them, prod them, motivate them, and even ethically bribe them to take action now.

Build in free bonuses that have a perceived high value, give a special discount for responding within 5 days, tell them all the problems they'll have if they don't do something now, etc.

And add a P.S. that restates your main benefit(s), your guarantee, or deadline for special offers...and always ask them to act now.

Okay, let's wrap this up.

Using these little secret techniques is the way to get your prospect/customer's attention so that they'll be ATTRACTED to your ad (first), then they'll be given the chance to develop a DESIRE for your product/service by seeing the BENEFITS to them that will lead them into WANTING your product/service enough for them to TAKE ACTION and BUY.

Remember your headline, ad, and sales letter are nothing more than...

"Salesmanship In Print."

(go on to the next chapter now)

Chapter Five...

"How To Communicate Your Sales Message So They Will Take Buying Action Now!"

Wouldn't it be great if everytime you write a letter or an ad, you knew the easy way to get your targeted prospect to take action and respond to your offer?

Did I hear you say, "Yes!"

Well, you've come to the right chapter.

An interesting point...

All of us --- you, me, and everyone you know --- always make decisions based on emotions, and then justify (and even defend) our decisions with logic.

You must communicate to people's emotions first, and then give them the "reasons why" to help them justify (and defend) their decisions with logic.

This my friend, is...

"The Key To The Vault!"

Do you remember, in an earlier chapter I said that I'd explain why people act the way they do because it's a fact of our biology?

Good, let me share with you a little secret.

You may not realize this, but you actually are three times smarter than you think you are?

You see, you don't just have one brain.

You actually and physically have...

"Three Brains!"

And the sooner you understand the role of each of your brains, the quicker you'll be able to communicate your sales message to your prospect and have them take action on your offer.

Okay, get comfortable and get ready for a fantastic journey inside your mind.

Your brain is actually three brains that have different functions and work together quite magically.

They are:

#1 - The "Thinker" Brain (Cerebral Cortex)

#2 - The "Mammalian" Brain (Limbic System)

#3 - The "Reptilian" Brain (Brainstem Functions)

Each of these brains have different ways of doing things, and more importantly to you, the marketer, have different ways that they process information and move toward action.

Let's start with The "Thinker" Brain.

The Thinker Brain is found in its highest developed form only in humans. And is located in what's called the Cerebral Cortex (you know, the grey matter).

That's about as scientific as we're gonna get here, so relax.

Anyway, this is where all of our conscious activity goes on. Our conscious thought processes, our logic functions, and all of our "upper level" thinking goes on here.

The Thinker Brain acts as the input processor. Sort of like the CPU on your computer.

It processes whatever is placed there. And it only works on one problem at a time (an important point to remember).

It's interesting that we humans take great pride in the ability to think logically, solve problems, and consider our Thinker Brain to be our greatest advantage.

However, it's really our weakest brain when it comes to motivations, it tires very quickly, and is subject to getting off course by "daydreaming" and sometimes just plain "going blank" on us.

It's in the Thinker Brain that we begin to become "aware" of a problem. By that I mean, the problem is registered here consciously for the first time, or it has been placed "on the front burner".

After the problem has been analyzed by the Thinker Brain, the most this brain will do is put it into the "need to" do something cubby-hole. It's not ready to take action, it's at the "Let Me Think About It First" stage.

Now a couple of observations.

Have you noticed that you can argue logically forever and ever, give every logical reason why someone should do something, have them logically agree with you along the way, and then they do absolutely nothing?

Have you heard them say, "Let me think about if first."

And have you ever heard someone say, "Yeah, I need to do that."?

An then they do nothing.

The reason they don't do anything is that you have communicated with the Thinker Brain whose role is to think logically, analyze logically, and unfortunately for you the marketer...who has mistakenly chosen to speak with the Thinker Brain first (instead of last)...this brain hasn't the self-motivation to take action on anything. It just likes to "think about it".

I call it the "Need To" Brain.

I "need to" do this...I "need to" do that.

But nothing gets done.

Obviously the Thinker Brain is not the brain to be talking with if you want someone to take action now.

Okay, let's look behind door number two...

49

The "Mammalian" Brain

The Mammalian Brain is found in mammals and other animals, and is located basically in the limbic system. Consider it your middle brain.

Here is where most all of your unconscious activity happens.

The best way to communicate with the Mammalian Brain is on a "touchy-feely" level.

Here is found our strong sense of belonging to groups, going along with social pressures, keeping up with the Jones, the me too, the lemming syndrome, and basically the "herd" or "group" mentality.

This Mammalian Brain is very personal and responds to the unchanging hopes and dreams of humanity, family love, and good feelings.

Now my marketing friend, we are getting somewhere!

This Mammalian Brain holds some promise, doesn't it?

But unfortunately for us, it's only able to move toward action, not take action.

I call it the "want to" brain. It "wants to" take action, but can't by itself.

"Before we go any further, let me warn you."

The information I'm about to reveal can be used in a wonderfully positive way to motivate people toward the good things in life, or unfortunately in the wrong hands, it can be used in absolutely the most negative ways to manipulate people toward the worst sides of human nature.

I continue writing here with the desire, understanding, and trust that you will choose to use this information only to motivate people toward the good things in life, and not for the purpose of negative manipulation.

Remember, a proposition is only truly good if it is a win-win-win for everybody involved.

Let me now introduce you to the marketer's "key to the vault".

The "Reptilian" Brain

The Reptilian Brain is found in all animals and in humans is located in the Brainstem and controls all of the brainstem automatic functions.

This is where all "Preconscious Activity" happens. All the preconscious experience that is programmed into us from generation to generation to generation and on and on.

This Reptilian Brain is always working!

It is our STRONGEST brain!

It is always asking only one question, "Is This Safe?"

Trying to decide "automatically" whether to stay or leave.

The Reptilian Brain is "The Gatekeeper" to the upper brains. All information is processed here first by asking the one question, "Is This Safe?" And then it is passed on to the other brains for group and logic comparisons.

This low level brain creates chemical changes in us. I'm sure you've felt the "adrenaline pump" you've gotten after being startled or been in an emergency situation (an emotional and instinctual response!).

The Reptilian Brain is only...Self Interest and Survival Motivated!

And the most important attribute of the Reptilian Brain is that it is the center for...

"Emotional and Instinctual Responses!"

You now know The Supreme Decision Maker, The Ultimate Authority For Taking Action, The Fast Facilitator, The..."I Gotta Brain"...whose singular job is to decide immediately whether to take action now, or send the information to the "higher" brains for justification using logic and group functions.

You have just been introduced to the A C T I O N brain!

Now it's much easier to see why the words YOU, YOURS, NEW, HOW TO, and FREE are so effective in marketing!

You are talking directly to the ACTION brain that is self interest and survival motivated, that is always asking "so what?...who cares?... and what's in it for me?", and is always asking, "Is This Safe?"

Now your job as a marketer is to develop your skills to communicate with this brain.

And the only way you can possibly communicate to a brain that works on immediate emotion and instinctual response is to...

"Appeal To The Emotions!"

That's why you use ATTENTION-GRABBING headlines that speak in terms of the BENEFITS to your prospect with STRONG GUARANTEES that provide SAFETY so that they are comfortable in TAKING ACTION!

You always want to be speaking first to the ACTION (reptilian) brain and let it make its decision to TAKE ACTION first, and then provide the THINKER and MAMMALIAN brains with the information they need to JUSTIFY the EMOTIONAL DECISION TO TAKE ACTION that has already been dictated by the ACTION BRAIN!

Let's sum this up...all of us --- you, me, and everyone you know --- always make decisions based on emotions, and then justify (and even defend) our decisions with logic.

You must communicate to people's emotions first, and then give them the "reasons why" to help them justify (and defend) their decisions with logic.

This my friend, is...

"The Key To The Vault!"

(go on to the next chapter now)

Chapter Six...

"How To Make The Buyer Feel Comfortable In Purchasing From You The First Time!"

The reason most people are hesitant of doing business with you the first time is that they don't know you personally, don't know anyone who does know you, don't yet trust you, or they feel completely at risk with their hard-earned money.

So how do you overcome this seemingly insurmountable obstacle?

May I suggest that you completely reverse the risk to the prospect.

In other words...

"You, the seller, take all the risk... instead of your customer."

Now you may think that I'm nuts.

Please hold your judgment for a moment.

Let's look at this, as always, from your customer's point of view.

Let's say you were in the market for a nice, late-model used car.

You drive into the car dealership and are greeted by a cordial salesman, who after letting you browse around for a while, suggests that you test drive the car that you're interested in.

So off you go and sure enough, this one seems like just the thing you've been looking for.

And when you get back, you sit down (in that little cubicle) with the salesman and go through all the regular car sales stuff and finally come together on a deal.

And you're ready to sign and then you see it...

THIS CAR SOLD AS IS --- NO WARRANTY

Do you think you might just hesitate a little or tell the salesman, "No Deal."

Now let's contrast this with the dealership down the street.

Same browsing, same test drive, same regular car sales stuff.

And then the salesman offers you this written guarantee...

"If for any reason at all, you're not completely satisfied with the purchase of your car, just bring it back within 30 days and will fix it, or if you wish, we will refund 100% of your money. It's your choice. And we'll even pay for the gas that you've used during the month."

Which car dealer would you buy from?

The second one for sure, right?

Now do you think he gets some people who would bring their car back to him during the month? And he may be making some repairs, and even possibly refunding some money?

Yes.

However, do you think his sales and profits are going through the roof because of this guarantee?

YES!

Why?

Because he has effectively taken the risk out of buying a car from his dealership.

And it makes the car buyer feel comfortable in making the purchase.

Now what can you learn from this little story.

First, you must stand 100% behind your product/service.

Offer to your customers a 100% money-back guarantee, that if for any reason they aren't absolutely delighted with what they have received, that you will return 100% of the money back to them.

Now you can put time limits to this, but I would recommend the longer the guarantee the better.

Are you not sure that you're comfortable in giving this strong of a guarantee?

Shame on you.

There are only two reasons why anyone should buy from you...

1. You're going to solve their problem

2. You're going to make them feel better

And if you're not doing one or both of these for your customer, then you don't deserve their money.

You should strive to have all happy customers by providing the best possible service and products.

And you should never keep anyone's money who is unhappy with your
product/service.

Are you going to have some who return for a full refund?

Sure. Some people won't see the full value that you have offered them. That happens.

But are you going to have a lot more sales because you're offering your risk-reversal, 100% money-back guarantee to your prospects?

I know so.

Do you?

Good.

How about giving them some free bonuses that they can keep even if they return your product/service for a refund?

That's what is called a "better-than-risk-free money-back guarantee".

Here's my best advice.

Sell your product/service with a 100% money-back guarantee with the longest free return you possibly can, and your sales will skyrocket because...

"You, the seller, take all the risk... instead of your customer."

(go on to the next chapter now)

Chapter Seven...

"The Most Effective Words In Marketing That Get Fast Results Over And Over Again!"

In an earlier chapter I gave you a couple of lists of words that have been used by successful marketers over the last hundred years.

n this chapter I'll be giving you words and phrases that you can use as is, or modify and add to, to attract interest and create desire for your product/service.

"That Magic Word...FREE"

If you take a while to study the offers that come to your Email and mailbox each day you'll see that the most effective marketing word of all time is FREE.

Here are some ways to phrase your free offer.

Yours free

Free trial offer

Free gift

Free to new members

Booklet free

Free examination

Ask for free report

Free demonstration

Literature free

Free consultation

Moneymaking facts free

Try it 10 days free

The next most popular thing that people want is to know, "What's New."

Here's how you can phrase news offerings.

At Last

New Method

New

Latest Findings

It's Here

Just Off The Press

New Discovery

Just Out

New and Improved

Beginning March 17

New Invention

Important Development

The World's First _____

Just Published

And people are always wanting to know how to do things...how to get something...how to solve their problems...how to make more money...how to have more fun in their life.

This one's sort of fill in the blanks.

How to _____   How to avoid _____

How to get _____   How to get rid of _____

How to have _____   How to end _____

How to keep _____   How to stop _____

How to start _____   How I _____

How to begin _____   How I improved my _____

How to become _____   How to enjoy _____

How to improve _____   How you can _____

How to develop _____   How to make _____

People are hungry for information. They buy magazines, read newspaper, watch the news, listen to the radio. Here's how you can tap into people's desire for information.

10 ways to _____   The truth about _____

20 tips for _____   What you should know about ____

Guide to _____   Advice to _____

Practical hints on _____   Fact you should know about _____

Plain talk about _____   Mistakes you can avoid _____

An interesting problem sometimes comes up. You are making an absolutely true statement, but because your reader may not have heard of such a thing before, the statement is unbelievable, even though it's true.

Here's a few ways to make your offer believable.

Award winning

Over 1 billion sold

Founded 1937

Here's what others say...

Established 17 years

Money back if not delighted

You risk nothing

Proven in laboratory tests

If not delight, just write cancel on the bill

You be the judge

People are always looking for a "good deal". Here's a few tips to phrasing yours.

Sale priced

Fantastic savings

Price going up soon

Only 10 percent above cost

Save up to $1000.00

Price going up on May 1st

Less than half price

Never again at this low price

Here's a "grab bag" of various phrases that can be used to fit circumstances.

Send no money

The key to _____

No obligation

Only $1 a day

Special offer

Now you can _____

Money-saving offer

Buy direct and save

The secret of _____

For quick information, call _____

Easy payment plan

Yours if you can qualify

No salesman will call

You don't risk a dime

Yours for the asking

As I've said before. Most people will procrastinate and put off making decisions about anything and everything. You must urge them to action and give them the reasons why they should do so.

Here's some phrases that have proved effective over the years.

Act now

Act fast

Don't delay

Be the first

Order now

Rush name for details

Order today

For a short time only

Order now, pay later

While supply lasts

Don't put it off

Price going up

Send today

Supply limited

Get started today

Last chance

When writing your messages, ads, sales letters to your prospects, come back to this section for inspiration and ideas.

Don't pass these words and phrases as overused. They are used because they work.

Remember to always put some YOU...NEW...and HOW TO into your offers.

And make sure that you ask the person to take action now.

It's been said a long time ago..."Ask And You Shall Receive".

Well, if you want action from your prospect, then you should be sure to...

"Ask For Action."

(go on to the next chapter now)

Chapter Eight...

"The Three Magic Words That Will Build Your Profits For Years To Come!"

Congratulations, we've come a long way together!

From finding the market who's hungry.

To writing your message in headlines, direct response ads, sales letters, etc.

And by following up with your prospects until the right time when they are ready to buy.

Now all of this is real important because you've narrowed down your market step-by-step-by-step, until you now have buyers of your product/service.

This is your HOT---HOT---HOT list.

These people have come along with you on each step of your marketing, and bought from you and are now happy customers.

Now you're ready to make all of your work pay off BIG-TIME!

Did you know that's it's 20 times easier to sell existing customers than it is to sell to new prospects?

Why?

Because they like you, they trust you, and they like what your product/service has done for them.

All this makes it so much easier for you to do business with them time and time again.

And this is where you're going to make your big profits...year after year after year.

The three magic words that will build your profits for years to come are...

"Back End Sales!"

The "Back End" is where you're going to make your big money.

And it's one of the most jealously guarded secrets of any successful marketer.

It's actually such a simple concept, you see, once your customer buys from you, it's light-years easier to get them to buy from you again. And it's so much cheaper, because you don't have to spend so much time and money to develop the original attraction, interest, desire, and action.

There's basically three ways to work your back-end sales.

#1 - Reselling

Reselling is simply selling them the same thing they bought before.

For example, consumable products (like health and beauty products, car performance additives, etc., basically anything that is consumed and needed again on a regular basis), or reoccurring services (such as accounting/bookkeeping, writing services, consulting, etc.).

When looking for some product/service to market, always try to think of products/services that are "consumables" that need to be purchased and used over and over and over again by your customer.

That in itself will give you tremendous back-end sales and profits.

#2 - Upselling

Upselling is getting your customers to buy a better, more expensive, or more up-scale products or services from you.

Let's say our friend Phil Phisher (the fly fishing expert), first gets his customers to buy his booklet on the secrets of fly fishing. And then, being the brilliant marketing maniac that he is, Phil offers his readers a fly tying kit, complete with all the necessary materials and instructions to learn to tie the flies themselves.

And for a little more they could see Phil tying the flies on a video that Phil produced for next to nothing (kind of home-spun, but still gets the information across just fine), with Phil giving thread by thread commentary on each twist of the process.

Then Phil offers them another course on how to use the flies that they have tied themselves in a manual (in book and audio) and video tape with Phil out there in the river with his waders on.

Phil has become quite a personality by now, hasn't he?

And you should too.

How about a seminar on fly fishing?

Or a special fly fishing dream vacation?

Can you begin to see how big this back-end thing is getting to be for Phil.

And all of this started with a little...

"FREE REPORT Reveals New Proven Fly Fishing Secrets"

Talk about acorns growing into oak trees, Phil now owns a whole forest!

Shoot, he could take this on forever by doing it all the same way again for each type of fish that his fishing fans want to catch.

What a concept!

#3 - Cross-Selling

Cross-selling is getting your customers to buy something else that's related to the original product/service that they purchased from you.

Let's see just how far Phil can go with this.

How about fishing rods, fishing reels, wading boots, caps, tackle boxes, camping gear?

And this doesn't have to be stuff that's got his name on it (although it certainly could).

Phil could "joint venture" with others who have already got quality products/services that Phil could market to his loyal following.

Do you think that there are other people who would love to have access to Phil's loyal fans?

Gracious sakes, yes!

"Does This Give You Any Ideas?"

Think about it for a minute.

What are some things that you can market as your back-end now?

What could you be selling to your customers that you aren't now?

Whose products/services could you use as back-end sales for you in a "joint venture" relationship?

Who could use your products/services as back-end sales in a "joint venture" relationship with you?

You could even market the products/services of other marketers who don't know that this can be done!

You don't even need to come up with a product yourself!

"Just Find The Market For The Products/Services...

And Create Joint Ventures With Others Who Have Already Produced The Products/Services!"

Okay, I digressed a little...so let's get back on track. You've got to begin to understand that the first sale that you make with your customer is just the beginning of a long lifetime relationship.

And it's very important for you to understand from the beginning the...

Lifetime Value of a Customer."

Let's say that your average new customer first buys something from you and it's worth $50 in profit. And over the course of the next three years (that's the average purchasing life of your customer in this example), they buy $100 worth...three times a year...with a $75 profit each time.

Now step back for a second and let's see what we got here.

A $50 profit on the front-end and $675 profit on the back-end (from $75 X 3 X 3).

"That's $725 of pure profit from each average customer!"

Now, let me ask you a question.

How much would you spend to get a customer that is worth $725 of profit to you?

Let's say that you could even break-even at $50 and still be very happy! (Or even more than $50!)

If you have a back-end in place that generates big profits you can easily afford to break-even, or...are you ready this one...

"Lose Money On The First Sale..."

because you know once they become a customer, they're worth $725 on the average to you.

You see, knowing the Lifetime Value Of Your Customer is a very valuable marketing tool.

One that deserves your time and attention.

And you can see it's important to plan your back-end, even if you're in the early stages of marketing to your marketplace.

You should always, always, always, be asking yourself what products/services you could sell, resell, upsell and cross-sell to your new customers and customers you already have.

I repeat myself to make this very important point.

"The Back-End is the most important part of your business and any business."

Don't have a short term outlook for your relationship with your customers.

Too many marketers only see the one sale on the front-end.

Don't you make that mistake.

Make sure that you're always thinking long-term.

Always be asking yourself, "How do you bring more value, more products, more services to your customers during their buying lifetime with you?"

How much would you invest in time and money into your marketing, if you knew that for every $50 you put into marketing, you would get back $725 in back-end profits?

Did I hear you say, "A lot!"

Right answer.

Just remember, your major investment into your business is always your front-end marketing to get your first sale with your customer.

After that, it's 20 times easier to make your sales through reselling, upselling, cross-selling and joint venturing with others.

Remember those three magic words...

"Back End Sales!"

(go on to the next chapter now)

Chapter Nine...

"How To Get More Marketing Ideas Than You Thought Possible!"

First let me congratulate you on two things.

#1 - Your decision to read and study this book and to come along with me this far.

This shows that you really are interested in your own success.

I know of too many people who will buy a book, begin to read a little of it, begin to skim, and then set it aside only to have it end up on the shelf with all the other books they've bought.

They never completely read a single book!

Most of them have only read the first chapter or two!

What a shame.

The printed word is the greatest thing that's ever happened to humanity!

It allows us to repeatedly have discussions with successful people, and learn from their mistakes and successes from hundreds and thousands of years ago, and from hundreds and thousands of miles away!

Just think of the accumulated wealth of knowledge that is available to you nowadays!

It's truly amazing, isn't it?

To be able to hear the hopes, dreams, fears, failures, and successes of the world's best thinkers, philosophers, inventors, statesmen, business visionaries, you name it.

I've found during my lifetime the quickest way to be successful at any venture or activity is to learn from the experiences, mistakes, and successes of others.

And learning through books and other information products is the very best way.

Learning from your own experiences can be a very painful waste of time and money.

#2 - You have invested in yourself.

There is no other investment on earth that will provide you a bigger pay off than investing in yourself. And I congratulate you for making your commitment to lifelong learning. So many people stop growing and learning after high school or college and just try to "tread water" through their lives.

Unfortunately for them, the world is changing at such an incredibly fast rate that they can't just "tread water".

In today's ever-changing world, you don't tread water...you either sink or you swim!

As in everything in life, you have a choice...

"You can ride the wave of technology... or be crushed by it!"

Congratulations on being high on the crest!

"Why marketing is the best investment you'll ever make."

If you learn to use it right, marketing can be the single, biggest, most effective profit-making tool that you can possibly use to boost and build your online business... and your profits!

Just think for a second...

You can put your money in the bank or buy some real estate and you'll get a return on investment of 5%, 10%, or even 20% annualized.

But by learning to use these effective marketing techniques in your online business, without a doubt, you'll get your biggest single return on your dollars, greater than any other place that you could think of.

"How come?" you ask.

Good question. The answer is actually very simple.

You see, a single ad, with the right headline, targeted to the right audience, with the right offer, costing only a few hundred dollars, can bring in returns of perhaps 1000% (or more) within days!

Now, just in your head, give that a quick calculation annualized over the course of a year.

What answer did you come up with?

That's right --- a lot!!

Now can you see why marketing is the easiest way for you to make more money in your business.

Here's a quick example...

Let's say you're already running an ad. And it's getting you 50 responses a week from it. And let's say you try a new headline (just a little variation) and now instead of 50 responses, you now get 80 a week.

And what if you could raise the number of sales you get from those 50 people who responded (by using a more effective presentation) from 20 to 30 sales, just ten more sale per week.

My friend and fellow entrepreneur, that's 520 more sales in one year.

Plus --- the extra ten sales that you get from the other 30 responses per week you're getting from the ad's better response. Put them together and...

Now you have 1,040 more sales per year!

Now let me ask you a question... How much extra profit did you just make for the same ad cost that you're spending right now?

Hmmn... interesting, isn't it?

That's what I call "The Magic of Marketing Leverage"... and you can use it too, in your business!

All you gotta do is try a few of these new ideas and experiment a little.

Try new offers, headlines, and targeted groups of people.

You'll be amazed at what it can do for your bottom line profits!

Now let me let reveal to you the magic ingredient that most people are missing in their recipe for success. This is the secret that will make everything happen for you and help you achieve all the dreams that you want for yourself and your family.

If I shout this secret loudly it will be drowned out by the noise of the unsuccessful masses.

Come close while I whisper...

"you must take action."

This is the only way you'll ever get what you want in life.

And here is a very important point...

"To get what you want in life, you must first help others get what they want in life. It's as simple as that."

And you, my marketing friend, must help others to... take action.

And as one of your first steps of action to becoming a successful marketer, you must commit yourself to be a lifelong student of marketing.

You must invest time and money to learn as much as you possibly can about marketing.

When I consult with business owners, one of my first questions to them is, "What business are you in?"

They invariably tell me they make this, or sell that, or provide a certain service.

I will then suggest that the business they just told me about is actually their second business...their first and foremost business is...

"The Marketing Of Your Business."

I don't care what business you think you are in, you are first in marketing.

Okay, so how do you learn more and more about this marketing business of yours.

I've got great news!

You can learn a whole lot of it for FREE!

(There's that very effective word!)

All you have to do is go to your mailbox everyday and get a wonderful education.

What do I mean, you ask?

It's what most Americans call "Junk-mail".

However, it's really "Gold In Your Mailbox"!

Start reading all of your junk-mail for the best marketing education that you'll ever get.

You say you hate getting junk-mail?

Did you know that the companies spend a fortune mailing those things out?

Did you stop to think that it must be profitable or they couldn't stay open very long?

Did you know that what you're seeing in your mail is the result of many tests that have been run and you're probably receiving the best pulling marketing package that the company has invested tens of thousands or millions of dollars to get to your mailbox and in your hands to read.

And did you know that those mailings are generating...

"Millions of dollars in business profits!!!

Like I said, "There's gold in your mailbox!"

Read it, save it, analyze it. Both the good...and the bad.

For a learning exercise, take the best parts of the best ads and paste them into parts of the weak ads. See what a difference it could make!

Now let's talk for just a minute about something of an online controversy.

U-mail...SPAM.

That's unsolicited mail or electronic junk-mail.

If you send out U-mail you can receive "flames" (nasty messages) from unappreciating people online. If you persist, you may even lose your online service with your provider.

In my opinion it's always better to market to people who have said they have an interest in your product/service instead of wasting your time and money on people who either are 1) not your market or 2) haven't discovered yet in their life's timeline, that they are.

One word of advice.

If you ever get a flame message, here's what to do.

First of all..."count to ten".

Delete their name from your E-mail Lists and put them on your Delete List.

Do not respond at all with a message back to them.

It will only escalate into an online shouting match.

Life's too short to deal with jerks. Leave them to themselves.

Go looking for positive people who want to make a better life for them and their families.

Now just because there are some people who don't appreciate U-mail, it doesn't mean that you can't appreciate it, does it?

You should learn to...

"Love U-Mail!"

It's the online equivalent of the "Gold In Your Mailbox" junk-mail in your postal mail box.

Read it, save it, study it, cut and paste it!

Plus you'll see all kinds, and I mean all kinds, of offers made online. It's quite an education in marketing a variety of products/services.

Learn from all of it.

"Get On Good Direct Marketing Mailing Lists!"

Anytime you see an example of great direct marketing writing, respond and get on their mailing list.

That will begin the flow of "priceless gold" to your mailbox you'll be able to "mine" for years to come.

A couple of the better direct marketing publishers are:

Boardroom Reports and Phillips Publishing

"Read magazines and study the headlines, stories and ads"

Did you know Reader's Digest has probably the most subscribers than any other publication?

And they TEST the headlines on the front wrapper of the copies you see at the grocery store checkout counter.

Do you think just maybe Reader's Digest has got their finger on the pulse of America, always testing to see what's gonna pull the most sales for their current issue?

The other great thing about Reader's Digest is the writing style they use. Human interest and easy reading. Those are traits you should emulate too.

Here's another magazine you always see at the grocery checkout counter...Cosmopolitan.

Just take a look at those headlines (well, okay, after you look at the girl).

My marketing maniac friend, those are GREAT HEADLINES.

They sell tons of those magazines each month.

And take a moment to analyze the topics...

Sex...Health...Money...Love...Weight Control... Did I Say Sex?

...all of the most common human desires.

And while we're at the grocery store checkout counter, don't forget to grab a copy of the...

"National Enquirer and Globe!"

Now just in case you think I've "flipped my pizza" (i.e. lost my mind), you should know that more Americans read these weekly magazines than they do the major newspapers combined!

Plus these guys are the masters at writing headlines with "news flavor" to them, and you'll see some great ads in these weekly rags in space ads and classifieds.

You may even find some ad ideas from the classifieds.

Remember, the successful ones run week after week after week.

Don't ever forget that average Americans go to the grocery store and these marketers know it!

Another place to get great ideas is the magazines called "Entrepreneur" and "Success".

Both are highly recommended.

"Start An Idea File"

Okay, now you've got all this information coming to you, you need to start an idea file.

Begin collecting great ads and sales letters, e-ads and u-mail, order cards, etc.

One way to learn to write in an effective direct marketing style is to write out great ads and sales letters that you find in long hand. That's right...by hand.

Why? ... Because the words will flow through you and you'll create a sensibility that the writer of the ad or letter had.

What you're trying to do is learn the technique of...

"Creative Emulation!"

By that I mean, learn to model (not steal or plagiarize) their success as your own.

You'll learn to recognize and use winning formulas and formats.

You've heard this before, but I'll say it again to emphasize my point...

"Don't reinvent the wheel!"

Another thing you want to be doing is sending for information and buying others people's products whose marketing is effective.

First to see what they deliver and what your competition may be like. And to see how they market to you to get the first sale...and after the original sale.

Remember how I said in an earlier chapter that it was your responsibility to say things in a number of ways for your reader to be able to understand the benefits you're trying to convey. Well, as you gather experience you also want to learn from a variety of sources and perspectives. You'll be able to transfer ideas from one market to another.

As a matter of fact, some of your best marketing ideas may come from one industry that you can apply to another.

Okay, I've given you a lot of ideas on how to get a whole bunch of study materials to start with. Thanks for coming along on this marketing journey.

(go on to the next chapter now)

Chapter Ten...

"How You Can Use The Most Powerful Marketing Secret Ever Devised To Generate A Steady Flow Of Qualified And Receptive Leads!"

In the never-ending search to come up with effective ways to market on the Net, here is the most effective I've found.

No, it's not sending "junk" email...and it's not putting ads in the "bulk-email ad pages" disguised as a newsletter with 5% news and 95% ads. And it's not even posting ads on AOL, CompuServe, you name it.

It's simply using the Power Marketing Principle of "Reciprocation".

Most all successful people realize they have gotten ahead in life by being helped along the way by others...by you helping others along the way.

That's right, read that again...

"you get ahead in life by being helped along the way by others... by you helping others along the way."

Now if you wish to gain the help of a lot of people what must you do first?

You must help more people yourself, FIRST.

Help others with their "word-of-mouth" marketing.

You KNOW it's the most effective kind of advertising there is.

The reason...it implies an endorsement to the referral by the referring party, and lets the relationship between the two new parties develop so much faster, building trust earlier in the new relationship.

And it's been said that no one will do business with you until they first...

"know you...like you...trust you."

They first must know who you are (awareness), like you (attraction), and trust you (feel that you are working in their best interest and providing more value to them instead of yourself).

How do you encourage this "reciprocal" concept?

You do it first!

Find someone, something, some company, that you truly like a lot and tell others about it. And then drop the person/company a note that you've been actively telling others about their product/service.

Ask them if the have a system for generating "word-of-mouth" referrals (most will not have clue what you're talking about, but they will be intrigued. I haven't found too many who don't want more business---in less time---for less outlay).

Tell them how you go about it (like what you're reading here) and let them know that you appreciate all the reciprocal "word-of-mouth" you can get also.

Will all of them cooperate with you? No, but you keep telling people about their good service anyway, over-loading up your side of the scales, you'll find someone else to help balance up your "scales of reciprocity" soon.

And when you find a few, lookout, here comes the inquiries.

You will be "endorsed by association" and the "know...like...trust" process has sped up incredibly.

How can you do this on the Net?

Share interesting email with others. Send out a "Neat Things I Found This Month On The Net" letter to your friends---listing newsletters to receive, websites to visit, mailing lists to subscribe to...and on and on. Just give a brief description of each and how to contact or subscribe. It doesn't have to be long or fancy, just from you to them, "upfront and personal".

On your website have a "links" to other sites page with descriptions on it so your visitors have a way to move around without having to search for what they are interested in. Plus, you will already have weeded out the junk and posted the really good stuff on your page.

Then, let the people/companies know that you actively provide "word-of-mouth" marketing for them and ask them to visit your website or read your "Interesting Stuff On The Net" to see their listing you did for them FREE...and ask politely for a "reciprocating" kind word or listing at their site too. And have them contact you for more info on a special "referral system program" you know about.

Like I said, some will, some won't. But the ones who do will increase your flow of leads, traffic, and new business beyond your wildest dreams.

And how much does this cost?

Just your willingness to recognize that...

"you get ahead in life by being helped along the way by others... by you helping others along the way."

Try it, it really works!

(go on to next chapter now)

Chapter Eleven...

"The Most Important Technique You Must Master BEFORE Setting Up A Web Page"

If you stop to think about it for just a minute, what is it that all nternet online users have in common that they can share?

I mean, we all have different computers, modems, software packages, internet providers, different levels of expertise...but there is one common thread that we all have access to.

That's right.

The single common thread that we all can use and share is...

>>> Email <<<

There are all levels of computer users online, and all with different levels of ability to get information up onto and off the Net. So one of my major points is that your marketing should be geared FIRST to the lowest common denominator that all Internet users can access, and that my friend, is email.

Then, and only then, should you transfer your SUCCESSFUL email to the other marketing technologies that are available to online marketers.

You absolutely have to get a handle on putting your sales message down into a email format that proves, over time and testing, to be effective and profitable...BEFORE you spend money and time with the larger mediums.

To be able to sell anything online, you have to use this bottom-line tool, email.

Email's greatest advantage is that it's quick, you can edit and paste, if something doesn't work you can change it and test it again very quickly, and most off all it's very inexpensive to send out your email to 1, 10, 100, 1000, 10,000, 100,000 or more people at one time.

What a concept!

You can use it effectively for "follow-up" on your prospects, nurturing them along to respond to your offer by repeated emails and follow-up offers.

Remember, you should at least follow-up three times to a prospect, probably with the same initial sales letter so they will become familiar with you.

Then start sending out different things from time to time, kind of trying out some "new bait".

Of course, repetitive email sent to prospects is the way to convert them to new customers. But, as a reminder, who is the easiest prospect for new business?

You remember well...the people who are already your customers.

They know you, trust you, and like you and your products/services. They've already been through the prospect conversion process to become your customer.

It's so much easier, quicker, and more profitable for you to ask them to buy more of your products/services than to spend all of your time and money chasing and trying to convert new prospects.

Now I didn't say you should stop prospecting for new customers, did I?

No, you always need a fresh stream of new customers, but my point is...don't ignore the goldmine that you have by "re-marketing" your products/services and NEW products/services to your current customers.

So I encourage, implore, nag, and prod you to go back and look through all of your email marketing pieces and test different headlines (yes, even your sales letters should begin with a headline --- NOT your name or company logo --- your name or company logo does not provide the prospect/customer with any benefit to them), different opening paragraphs, different closes.

Test different offers, guarantees, different free bonuses, different prices, a different P.S. after your signature signoff. Test each and every variable SEPARATELY so you can methodically find which one change will provide you with the best results for each ad or sales letter you do.

Use the techniques that are in the chapters of your copy of "How To Make Your Ads, Sales Letters, and Websites Sell Like Crazy" book. Go back and re-read the chapters frequently. This is not a book you just go through once. Refer to it each and every time you're putting an ad, letter, posting, or web-page together...and use the secrets that have been tested and proven to your benefit.

Okay, let's wrap this up.

Work very hard at making your email bring you profitable results. By using email to test and test and test, until you find your winning combination, then you're ready to "roll-out" your offer to more and more people through the other e-marketing avenues.

(go on to next chapter now)

Chapter Twelve...

"How To Put Your Online Business On A "No-Brainer... Auto-Pilot... It-Does-The-Work-While-You-Goof-Off" System"

In the last chapter we talked about how you should become a crackerjack at using email to market your products/services before moving on to more advanced online marketing tools.

Well, now we're going to talk about the first step you should take into putting your online marketing business on a "No-Brainer...Auto-Pilot... It-Does-The-Work-While-You-Goof-Off" System.

The first step, before moving onto webpages, is to set up your email "sales machine" on a AutoResponder system.

This my friend, is the online marketers dream come true.

You'll be able to have people request more information from your ads, address their email request to your AutoResponder's address, and have your AutoResponder email the information out to them AUTOMATICALLY for you, without you have to lift a finger (or even know that it just happened).

You can literally put your online business on AutoPilot!

An AutoResponder is basically an "automatic" robot that has a specific email address.

When an AutoResponder receives an email message, it immediately returns the requested information (special report, sales letter, follow-up letter, order form, etc.) to the email address of the person requesting your information.

AutoResponders are set up on computer systems that are ready and ever-so-willing to receive messages from the Internet community...24 hours a day!

So you never "close your doors" to customers.

You're always open for business!

You are accessible, through your AutoResponder, anytime, morning, noon, and night, every day of the year.

Here's a few ideas of how you can use an AutoResponder to help out with your online marketing chores.

When you place e-ads or newsgroup messages, there are sometimes limitations on how much you can say about your product/service in that small posting to actually do the SELLING --- remember the more you tell, the more you sell.

So you've got to have a way to get more information about your offer out to your prospect.

When doing the "manual labor" of online marketing, you would tell your prospect to send you an email message at your email address and request the Special Report or information that was offered in your e-ad or posted message. Then you would manually retrieve your email, compose mail, reply to their request, and send it out to them whenever you get around to it.

Those days are gone!

With an AutoResponder you don't have to do this. Instead of having your prospect send their request for more information to your email address, you have them send their request for more info to the email address of your AutoResponder.

Your "always-working, never-complaining" little AutoResponder will send them your Special Report that they've requested in about a minute by email. You don't have to be online, you don't have to check your email to retrieve information requests, you don't have to manually compose mail to send out to each prospect...and your prospects don't have to wait for you to get back to them later on, they get the information now, while they are thinking about it. Your prospects do not have to wait for you to get back online to learn more about what you are selling.

Remember that we humans can only have one thing "on our front-burner" at a time. If someone is thinking about you now, you want to be able to deliver the information they want before they move you to the "back-burner" of their mind, where you become just another one of a thousand things that they had wanted to get around to some day, but something else has now made it the "front-burner".

In our "Instant" Society, when someone reads your e-ad or message, and requests more info...they want the info now, not 24 hours later. Your AutoResponder will get it to them...and fast.

Probably the greatest thing about your AutoResponder is that you'll get the email addresses of each and every person who requested info from your AutoResponder (this service is available depending upon who you select as your AutoResponse provider).

This is the one thing you're really after.

You'll be able to follow-up with your new found prospect with other messages, reports, and updates to nurture them along to become a long time customer of your products/services.

One of the most valuable marketing secrets is to track where your prospects are seeing your initial ad or message that they have responded to. That way you know the results of your ads and can make changes and improvements to responses and get more "bang for your buck" invested. You'll know where the best places to advertise are...and where not to waste your time and money.

Your AutoResponder can do just that for you...automatically. You'll know that from ad#1 all requests went to AutoResponder#1 and so on. So you can track and measure your results, so you can continually improve your marketing results and profits.

If you direct your prospects requests to your webpage first, then you don't know which ad they saw and you have no way of tracking and improving your ads for greater profits and free time...which is the name of the game.

Or how about if you have folks who need information from you that is continually being updated, like a price list, press releases, catalogs, current inventory availability, you name it. You simply update your AutoResponder when your information changes and your prospects and customers can always have the most recent information at their "beck and call" 24 hours a day.

Now if you do already have a webpage, I'm not saying get rid of it.

No, no, no.

Add one, two, or more AutoResponders to it so that your webpage visitor can get more info from you by email so they can read it thoroughly, print it out, touch and feel it, and spend some time with your info and offer of products/services.

And the greatest benefit to you for having an AutoResponder(s) linked to your webpage is that you'll be able to get their email address after they ask for more info from your AutoResponder...so that you can add them to your emailing list for further follow-ups and offers.

I think you can see by now, an AutoResponder can really help you out in making your online marketing more time efficient and profitable. And the best part is you can rent AutoResponders for only a few bucks a month.

What kind of things should you look for when shopping around for an AutoResponder provider?

Here's a few tips...you should be able to get unlimited incoming requests and unlimited outgoing replies, you should be able to update your information whenever you want without extra charges, there should be no setup fees, and you'll want them to provide you with the email addresses of each person who requests info be sent to them for your own follow-up.

Okay, let's wrap this up.

Your AutoResponder will save you time, save you money, and help you make more sales than ever before.

The time saver --- your prospects can contact you for more info 24 hours a day, while you're asleep or out doing things that you want to be doing instead of cutting and pasting email for hours a day. Your AutoResponder can handle literally THOUSANDS of requests for your information to your prospects and customers... there's no way that you have enough time in the day to manually deal with this kind of volume, and your AutoResponder "robot" can do it all for you, without you even lifting a finger.

The money saver --- just think for a minute about how much it really costs to follow-up with a prospect to get the sale. You may have long distance calls to them, toll-free 800 calls back to you, printing, postage, mailroom costs...this can really add up fast.

Now this is just your expense, how about your customers? You can have your prospects call in long distance on your FAX-ON-DEMAND line and get your info, but they pay for the phone...good for us, bad for them.

By requesting info from your AutoResponder, they receive your info for FREE, and everybody likes to get for FREE, don't you?

The great sales-producer --- your prospects and customers want information...right now...from you, while they're thinking about it. You know that you lose a lot of sales because you don't have your message their when they are ready and willing to buy. With your little "Sales Robot" AutoResponder, you'll be able to make those impulse sales when people are ready to buy.

And as I've said before, you'll be able to get the address of each person who requests more info on your products/services for further follow-up.

It's been discovered that it takes...on average...7 contacts with someone new before they will do business with you.

Most people don't make buying decisions that first time they hear from you.

It takes a slow and nurturing approach to convert prospects into clients these days. Especially, when marketing online, where you can't see each other face-to-face in person.

Here's a few ways to use your AutoResponder in your marketing.

Put your AutoResponder address in your "Signature" (or in a P.S. after your signature) at the end of your e-ads or newsgroup messages so that people who are interested in hearing more about your info can request more info and receive it instantly from your AutoResponder.

Most of the time, when you place ads online, it's hard to make them long enough to completely explain the benefits of your offer to your prospect/customer. That's why you should be able to provide them with more information from your AutoResponder.

Your webpage could be your Special Reports "clearinghouse", where each visitor could request your Special Report(s) from your AutoResponder. This will make your webpage much more time efficient (one of the visitor's biggest complaints about webpages, "they take too long, so I don't wait around to see what's there") and useful to your visitor.

They'll be able to read your info they receive from your AutoResponder offline, saving them time and money, and spend more focused energy with your offer.

From your own experience you know that while bouncing from webpage to webpage, people are usually just browsing...not buying.

And of course, and I repeat myself once again (I just can't emphasize this enough), by having them request your info from your AutoResponder, you will be able to get your webpage visitors' email address for future follow-ups.

You can even put your AutoResponder email address on your print ads and sales pieces so that your prospects can access you from any Internet provider and know how to get your info fast.

I could go on and on, but I think you understand already how valuable AutoResponders can be to you and your prospects/customers in the marketing of your products/services online.

(go on to next chapter now)

Bonus Chapter 1...

"Emotional Response Direct Marketing"

You remember me saying...

"The Marketing Technology Has Changed... But Human Hopes And Desires Do Not."

What I mean by that is people still want all the same things out of life that they always have. You know, safety, security, shelter, love, friends, belongings, sex, money, power, recognition, fun, good times, laughs, excitement, you name it.

All of these are basic parts of being human.

And you've learned from me, and others most likely, that all humans make decisions emotionally, and then, rationally justify those decisions with logic.

Therein lies our problem to solve.

Most people are rushed for time these days.

They tend to want to just get to the bottom line...like NOW.

The problem with that is you never, I mean NEVER, can sell anything to anybody by dropping to the "bottom line" immediately without first describing the benefits to the buyer and building value and DESIRE for your product or service.

By dropping to the bottom line too soon, you risk that the buyer won't really appreciate the true value and benefits that you're really offering them, or will completely miss your point that you're trying to make altogether.

You've got to lead them through this process... Step By Step By Step.

Also, you're trying to get your reader to invest in your relationship by spending his/her time with you. This raises that odds of making an EMOTIONAL tie with your reader.

Now some of your may think that people just won't take the time to read a whole bunch of information.

Well, I'm here to tell you that they will, IF it's interesting, beneficial to them, and not BORING!

Think about the things you're interested in. When you send away for information, you want to know as much as possible before you make a buying decision, don't you?

And you want to feel like you at least have some sort of good feelings about the person who is making the sales offer...a HUMAN EMOTIONAL CONNECTION of a sort.

Now if that's the way you go about making buying decisions, don't you think other "humans" do the same? Sure they do.

Now the best way I've found to do this is to write a LOT of information based on the BENEFITS to your reader and from the READER'S point of view.

So how do you go about doing this?

Start making a list of the problems that people have in relation to the topic of your product/service.

These are all of the "pains-in-the-neck" human emotional hot-buttons that you can use to present the problems that your reader is having and show your empathy and understanding of their feelings and present position.

Then make a list of all the benefits that your product/service offer to your reader.

These are the SOLUTIONS to their problems and all the good things that they'll have when they follow your advice or buy your solution to their problems.

Now you have two lists.

Begin with the first list of problems and weave a "human interest" type of story about real people who are having these problems that your reader can relate to and hopefully become emotionally stirred by saying to themselves, "Boy, that's just like me."

Then proceed to weave in how things could be so much better by applying the secrets that you have to reveal to them and go into the benefits that your solutions offer to them.

And then move on to your "sales pitch". But only after they have been "primed" a little with the background of the problems and how things could be so much better by following your lead.

Your project to work on: go back through your ads and sales letters to see if you're spending enough time to get your reader involved emotionally before you go for your sale.

(go on to next chapter now)

Bonus Chapter 2...

"The Simple Little Secret That Will Improve Your Success Exponentially"

Have you happened to notice that most people just don't respond to your offers the first time?

Did I hear you say..."YES!"

Now, of course, some respond immediately, don't they.

But you know as well as I that it takes more contact than just once to get most people moving (like 99% of them).

And as you make more contacts (repetitions of your offer), you get more and more business. It's been shown that it takes AT LEAST 7 contacts with you before you have established yourself in the mind of your prospect.

So each step of the way, you get more and more business as your message finally makes it to the "front burner" in your prospects life...and they respond by accepting your offer and doing business with you.

But what do you do with the ones who don't buy or do business with you?

What do you do with the ones who contact you back and ask you to remove them from your list of interested prospects, even though they said they WERE interested in your offer and information...just a short time ago?

Have you ever heard this phrase?

"When life hands you a lemon, just add sugar and you've got lemonade."

Napoleon Hill, the great success researcher and author of "Think and Grow Rich", probably best summed up this principle a few years ago when he wrote...

"Every adversity, every failure, and every heartache carries with it the Seed of an equivalent or a greater Benefit."

So what I'm suggesting to you is that, yes...it's very important to get customers/clients from your offers of products and services...but don't overlook the GOLDMINE that the people who don't buy from you represent.

I know, I know...a lot of you here are thinking I've gone off the deep end again. As always be patient with me.

Let me explain by example...

A few days ago I received an email from Joe (not his real name) requesting that his name be removed from our email list...and yes...he HAD requested the information be sent to him a few months ago. Why did he ask to be taken off...don't know.

But he had written a short note with it and seemed like a nice fellow, so we deleted his name from our list as he requested and he won't be receiving any more messages or offers from us.

However, I did send him back a personal email note just to let him know that his name had been removed from our list...and asked him for a small favor.

It went like this...

Dear Joe:

Just a quick note to let you know that your name has been deleted from our email list.

Thanks for your nice note.

Joe, I'd like your help.

If you could take just 30 seconds and let me know exactly what was it that you WERE looking for when you initially requested information from us, I'd really appreciate it.

It really helps to get feedback from customers...and more importantly, people who did not buy what you are offering.

Thanks in advance for your help.

You will not receive any further messages from us.

Sincerely,

Mark Hendricks
Hunteridge, Inc.
P.O. Box 753
Trilby, FL 33593
Voice: 352-583-3697
Email: mark@hunteridge.com

=== end of letter ==

Now did I take a little risk that this guy might get real mad at me for sending him another message?

Yes.

But a couple of things I knew before sending it to him...he did initially request information from me...I do give out in my sales letter a LOT of VERY VALUABLE information that, if he recognized the value, he's already been able to use and put money in his pocket...he did write a pleasant note requesting to be removed (not a burning nasty one)...so I thought he might be kind enough to help me out a little too.

Now he could have just deleted my message into "silicon oblivion"...but he didn't.

Here's his response (word for word)...

Mark:

I had just signed up and was looking around to acquaint myself with the system.

Your ad hit my eye and I thought I would inquire.

My business is mainly buying accounts receivable and I am always looking for ways to market my business. My contacts are basically business selling to other business and I felt your draw is more for retail type marketing.

I may be wrong, but that is why I don't think your service was applicable.

Thank you for all your help and I wish you much success. Joe

=== end of letter ===

Nice letter, wasn't it?

Now one thing you have to remember (and I struggle with this all of the time myself) is that when Joe (or any other person gives you their reason for doing or not doing something...are you ready for this?...

THEY ARE ABSOLUTELY RIGHT!

Joe wrote back HIS thoughts (see the word "think")...and feelings (see the word "felt").

And to Joe, his thoughts and feelings are ABSOLUTELY RIGHT.

It's interesting that Joe used both the words "think" and "felt" in this letter, isn't it?

Remember in the article where you learned that your brain is really three brains...logical...emotional...instinctual.

Joe just gave you and I a REAL LIFE lesson in his letter back to me, didn't he.

He logically THOUGHT that our service didn't apply to his marketing situation and he FELT that our approach was more geared to retail products and services.

And let me say once again that in Joe's mind, he is ABSOLUTELY RIGHT and you must learn to believe that he is ABSOLUTELY RIGHT (more about this later).

HOWEVER...before I continue, let me say that I believe Joe has made a big mistake in "thinking" about his "business to business" marketing. And there is an...

>>> IMPORTANT POINT FOR YOU TO LEARN FROM JOE <<<

There is no such thing as "business to business" marketing... there is only...

"PERSON TO PERSON"..."HUMAN TO HUMAN" MARKETING !!!

Has a "business" ever signed a check? Has "business" ever called to order your product/service using their credit card? Has a "business" ever handed you cash?

NO!

A real live and breathing INDIVIDUAL HUMAN PERSON made the final decision (yes, maybe a committee had input to the decision, but the "top dog" has the final say-so) to purchase your goods or services and write that check (or have it written by the accounts payable department), or call you on the phone, or put cash into your from their hand.

Never has a "business" made any kind of a decision on anything...PEOPLE DO!!!

People that have...hopes...dreams...desires...problems...and all kinds of terrible things happening in their lives that are keeping them from getting all the positive things that they want out of life.

Throw away your LOGIC brain for a minute and let me talk to your ACTION brain for a second...your instinctual brain.

Real live and breathing humans will only respond (read "take action") with their EMOTIONS...never with their logic. The logical brain is only there to help justify and defend the already-made emotional decision to proceed by taking action based on the emotions of hope, dreams, desires of gain, and fears of loss.

Do you "think" I'm wrong? (a "logical" statement by the way)

How does the logical brain decide to think about something...there has to be some motivation to even begin thinking, doesn't there?

May I suggest to you that the logical brain gets its motivation to begin analyzing from the emotions which have already developed the DESIRE to begin moving in the direction of action and has asked the logical brain to justify this action that is about to happen.

I could go on and on, but I FEEL you get the point I'm making.

Emotions are what will motivate your prospect to do business with you...not logic...and you, my marketing friend, must market to people and their emotions...not to their logic or "business" image.

By the way, put on your marketing cap for a second...what problems and solutions do you think Joe's market of businesses (read "PERSON") need...Want...and GOT TO HAVE?

Remember he said he buys ACCOUNTS RECEIVABLES...why would some business (read "PERSON") want to sell their accounts receivables to Joe...accounts receivable are outstanding bills that people owe to the business (read "PERSON").

Do you think that maybe that business (read "PERSON") needs...Wants...or maybe just has GOT TO HAVE CASH NOW and is willing to sell those accounts receivables to Joe at a substantial discount to get the CASH NOW.

Do you think there are some HUMAN EMOTIONS involved here?

Have you ever needed...Wanted...HAVE GOT TO HAVE CASH NOW to pay a few bills to SURVIVE as a "business" (read "PERSON") or as a family, or individual?

Yea, I think there's a LOT of emotions that Joe could market right in the middle of and stir up to get the emotional and instinctual brains to over-ride the thinker brain in taking action to get him a TON of business with his prospects, don't you?

Okay. What exactly DID I constructively learn from Joe's letter.

1) that I obviously DID NOT show him that our marketing techniques were EXACTLY what he really has to have to make a connection in his "business to business" selling.

2) that I made the big mistake of trying to let him, the reader, interpret my message instead of making it easy for him to exactly see the immediate benefits he will receive from our services.

3) that I need to revamp my sales messages to specifically answer the question BEFORE someone begins "thinking" to themselves that this emotional marketing and relationship-based marketing is not for them because somehow they "think" their situation is "different" (i.e. "business to business", "unique" market, "upscale clients", high-end products, you name the reason/excuse).

So you can see, that I FULLY take responsibility for his not understanding what I was trying to offer him. It's not his fault that I didn't present my message clearly, is it?

No, it's my fault.

Now fortunately I've had a lot of people who DID respond and purchased my services and products...but just think of how many people that there may be out there like Joe that didn't buy because of something they "thought" instead of the emotions I could have made them "feel" by being more clear.

And Oh Boy what I learned in this particular situation by asking Joe that simple question that we used all the time when we were a little kid that served us so well, that little most powerful key to unlock all answers, just ask...

WHY?

It's simply AMAZING what you'll find out.

Soooo...here's Mark, who learned something from Joe, (a non-buyer, a "goldmine of feedback", a lemon to make lemonade, a seemed failure of a prospect who gave me the opportunity to have a seed for an equal or greater benefit, thank you Napoleon Hill) has been busily revamping ads, sales letters, and other marketing to make them even more effective at producing profits.

It's ever-evolving folks...a non-stop process...always fine tuning...to make your marketing work better and better and better.

The great thing is that you guys are all into so many different business areas, but you're finding that these marketing techniques can be used in any business and any medium, aren't you?

Why?

It's because you're marketing into people's emotions, getting their attention, and providing them with the things the want and HAVE GOT TO HAVE. And learning to keep after them (ever so gently) until they respond.

(go on to next chapter now)

Bonus Chapter 3...

"Get A FREE Lesson In Direct Response Marketing That's Worth Millions"

I've written about this before, but I still see a lot of our clients not taking advantage of millions of dollars of research into direct response marketing.

And it's FREE to you everyday!

All you have to do is walk to your mailbox and sit down with all of your so-called "junk-mail". (otherwise known to us who have learned from it as a goldmine of direct marketing research that's available for us to learn from and model).

Listen up, now.

As a reminder, those direct mail companies have spent thousands or millions of dollars to get that envelope into your mailbox. The smart ones have tested and tested and tested different headlines, openings, approaches, benefits, prices, response mechanisms, ways to order, guarantees, bonuses, PS's, colors, lift letters, envelope size, what's on the outside of envelope...you name it...they've tested it.

Cause they're spending a lot of $$$ in printing and postage just to get their offer into the hand's of their TARGETED LIST and if the mailing doesn't work, it isn't profitable, and they don't make money or stay in biz very long, do they?

And you. my friend, have got the chance to "go to school" off of them.

They've spent thousands and millions to test these variables and you can have the benefit of their testing to develop your own style of direct marketing pieces.

So how do you do this?

Save up all of your junk mail for a week...set down when you can have a block of time for thinking...read through the ones you have and pick one that is effective on you as a place to start.

Now go through and analyze just for a second the parts of the letter...the headline...the salutation...the opening paragraph...the building of interest and desire...the benefits and advantages...the offer...the guarantee...the bonuses...the time pressure...the limited availability...the signoff...the PS...and anything else you notice.

Just sort of take a pencil and mark on the letter these different areas of the letter so that you learn to recognize them.

Now here's the fun part...begin at the beginning of the sales letter on your word processor and type it all in...but rewrite it using your product or service...use their words and transitions where you can or change them up to match your style...but don't get away from it too far. But then again, don't plagiarize. You should be using what's called creative emulation.

Use their letter as a model for yours.

What you're going after here is to learn the formula for a successful sales letter.

They have spent a ton of $$$ to get those words into your hands and when big $$$ are involved, smart marketers don't like to take chances, they like to make $$$!

So give this a try and test your new salesletter against the one you've been using.

A Quick Example Of Restyling An Ad

Here's an real live example of how you can restyle an ad and make it more attractive to the eye (easier to read) and therefore more effective.

This came from one of my clients and it is used with permission..

Here's where we started with the ad...

= = = = = = = = = = = = = = = = = = = =

HOW TO AVOID THE 10 BIGGEST MISTAKES PEOPLE MAKE WHEN BUYING A HOME!!!

Buying a home and taking out a mortgage is probably the biggest financial decision in your life. If you make and one of the 10 biggest mistakes home buyers usually make, you could cost yourself thousands, or even tens of thousands, of needless taxes and interest expenses every year! Don't make a move without getting this FREE information, that will reveal the hidden secrets your banker, real estate agent and accountant will never tell you!! Visit www.get-the-info.com for complete info.

= = = = = = = = = = = = = = = = = = = =

I think you'll agree that he's given the reader a lot of reasons why he/she should respond and get this free report. There ARE a lot of little secrets that most homeowner buyers and homeowners don't know that the banks and mortgage companies would prefer us not to know about, and yes it is costing Americans a lot of money during your lifetime.

So what kind of changes did we make?

Well...here's the restyled version...

= = = = = = = = = = = = = = = = = = = =

At Last --- A New Special Report Reveals...

HOW TO AVOID THE 10 BIGGEST MISTAKES PEOPLE MAKE WHEN BUYING A HOME!!!

Buying a home and taking out a mortgage is probably the biggest financial decision in your life.

If you make just one of the 10 biggest mistakes home buyers usually make, you could cost yourself thousands, or even tens of thousands, of needless taxes and interest expenses every year!

Don't make a move without getting this Special FREE Report that will reveal the hidden secrets your banker, real estate agent and accountant will never tell you!!

To get your free copy of this special report, visit…

www.get-the-info.com

Sincerely,

His RealName
RealName Financial Group
Voice: 904-555-4321
Fax: 904-555-1234
Email: his-address@his-address.com

P.S. You may be tempted to put this off and not take action. Don't make that mistake. Your banker is praying that you don't see the jealously-guarded money-saving secrets revealed in this special free report. Email the message now while it's fresh on your mind.

= = = = = = = = = = = = = = = = = = = =

Comments: As you can see, we split the teaser ad into a few shorter paragraphs…makes it easier to read…and yes they will scroll down, if each time they scroll your information is interesting to THEM.

Also we set the headline so it looks like a headline, changed around just a few words, and made it easier to see how to respond to get the report.

Also gave it a "signature" with his name, company name, and how to get in touch with him every which way. (Except postal mail, tests have shown that people respond less when they see where you are geographically located in an initial ad…but always include it in your sales letter)

And…added a P.S. to the end to "push them into action" a little.

Some "Q and A"…

Question: Could you tell me a little more about what you mean by using "Think and Grow Rich" as a marketing tool?

Answer: Get out your copy of "Think and Grow Rich". go to page 197, which should be Chapter 12 - The Subconscious Mind.

You'll notice in this chapter, Napoleon Hill talks about the subconscious mind and the EMOTIONS that we all have (by the way for you FREEBIE readers, there's a whole chapter in the book that talks about how to get into the three brains of each of your prospects so that they will respond to your offers).

Here, Hill lists the seven major positive emotions:

desire...faith...love...sex...enthusiasm...romance...and hope

He also lists the seven major negative emotions (to be avoided):

fear...jealously...hatred...revenge...greed...superstition...anger

These, my marketing friend, are the ways to motivate a human being.

Please note. I did not say manipulate.

Motivation in my opinion is when you are helping someone in a positive way to benefit them.

Manipulation is when you use these techniques for your own purely selfish motives with no regard of the negative impact you may have on others.

I am NOT advocating the manipulation of people, that's not nice and morally and ethically wrong.

However, by understanding how the human emotions work in the buying process, you can help many, many people by getting them past their own inertia to finally take action to benefit themselves and their families.

Please motivate. Please DO NOT manipulate. Thanks.

Anyway...can you see that the first list of emotions are based on the desirable things in life...things that people want.

And the second list is things that people want to avoid.

People only take action when one of two things are present:

1) the possibility of gain (toward gain)

2) the avoidance of loss (away from loss)

And they will only TAKE ACTION if you can get them out of their "COMFORT ZONE" by stimulating their emotions...both in the gain and loss categories.

I encourage you to be a "student" of human emotions and actions for the next week (and the rest of your life). Learn how people actually make decisions.

Certainly, not logically do they (or you for that matter)?

The fact is that we all make our decisions emotionally and then justify our decisions logically later.

Observe everyone you come in contact with this week. Your family, your friends, your employees, your bosses, your customers, everyone. See how the go about solving there problems that come up and opportunities that they come across. You'll learn a lot about them and yourself.

(go on to next chapter now)

Bonus Chapter 4...

"Three Words Guaranteed To Make Your Sales Letter Fail...Get Rid Of Them And Watch Your Responses Skyrocket!"

When reviewing clients' ads, sales letters, brochures, and other sales pieces there are three words that always need to be deleted to make the letter more effective in generating responses.

Before you hear what the words are, let's make sure that you know where the emphasis of your ads or letters should be. The emphasis, of course, should always be on your customer.

You'll want to speak to your readers needs, wants, desires, and fears.

That's how you'll be able to get your message into your prospects' emotional level brain so that your customer will take action. Remember, all decisions are made on an emotional basis first and then justified by logic later.

And the best way to get to your prospects emotional brain is to speak of the benefits your customer receives by purchasing your product/service...not the features...but the benefits.

As a reminder, BENEFITS are the RESULTS your customer will receive by doing business with you and features are the distinguishing characteristics of your product/service.

It's great that your product/service has distinguishing characteristics (features) that separate you from your competition, however, if you show your prospect the desired RESULTS you can provide, then you're showing your customers the BENEFITS received by purchasing your products/services.

Okay, so what are these three words guaranteed to make your ads and sales letters fail?

They are the words that completely take the focus off of your customer...these three words do not speak to your customers' emotions...these three words do nothing to instill desire in your prospect for your product/service...the three words to get rid of in your ads and sales letters are, "I...Me...My".

These three words put the emphasis and spotlight on you, the writer, instead of your customer/prospect. There is no way for you to communicate to your reader's emotions if you only speak about yourself ("I, me, my"). You've got to be writing to your reader, about your reader and your reader's hopes, desires,. wants, dreams, and fears.

That's how you get them to respond to your offer.

Now here's something that you may find interesting.

Have you noticed that in this discussion, that the words "I, me, or my" have not been used?

YOU...have been the complete focus of this discussion...YOU and YOUR customers and prospects.

And at first it's pretty hard to get the words "I, me, my" out of your writing.

Why is that, you ask?

Well, it's because of...you guessed it...your own emotions.

All humans, "way down deep", are only interested in their own wants and desires. That's "way down deep" on the subconscious levels (remember the article about the three brains and how to communicate with each).

So that's why it's hard at first to get rid of these three words.

But fortunately for your bank account, you can learn to delete "I, me, my" from your vocabulary and learn to turn phrases into "you, your, and yours" that put the spotlight where it belongs, which is on your customer/prospect.

This one little change in your ads and letters will increase your effectiveness and your results immediately.

So here's what you do now.

Go through your ads and letters and re-write any sentence that has the words "I, me, my" in them. By doing this, you'll automatically have to place the spotlight on your customers, which will help you communicate the desired results (benefits) of your product/service to your customers own wants and desires.

Now sometimes it just seems impossible to get around using an "I, me, or my" in a sentence (but make sure you don't give up too easy). When this occurs, use the words "we, us, our" instead. This will soften the focus on "I, me, my" and give you a little springboard to get back to using the words "you, your, yours". But make sure that you've tried every which way to phrase the sentence using "you, your, yours" first.

Give it a try and YOU will see YOUR results skyrocket.

From YOURS truly,
Mark.

(go on to next chapter now)

Bonus Chapter 5...

"A Quick And Easy Way To Write Sales Letters"

A lot of the time in our Marketing Action Plan consultations with you, the topic of how to write a sales letter comes up, so here is a quick and easy way to write your sales letters, a template for your use.

1. Get your prospect's attention by using a big benefit headline

2. Let your reader know the advantages they receive from your product/service

3. Prove that you can deliver the advantages and results promised

4. Persuade the reader by appealing to their emotional wants, desires, and fears

5. Get them to take action now by making an irresistible offer

Okay, let's start with the headline.

Think of your headline is an "ad for your ad".

Your headline must generate enough curiosity and interest so your reader will read the rest of your letter. A great headline is AT LEAST 80% of your letter or ad. That's how important headlines are.

By testing different headlines, with the same letter, results have increased by as much as 1,700%!

That's how important headlines are to your success.

Always remember that people are always looking to move toward gain and away from pain. So headlines that show these benefits work over and over again.

Show the reader how they can be better off in areas of their life that are attractive or show the reader how they can avoid the negatives of life.

Here's some words that have appeared in some of the best-pulling ads of all time.

"Top 10 Words Used In The 100 Most Successful Headlines Of All Time."

```
you..................... 31
your.................... 14
how.................... 12
new.................... 10
who.................... 8
money................. 6
now.................... 4
people................. 4
want.................. 4
why.................... 4
```

By the way, did you notice how many times the works YOU and YOURS appeared?

Like we discussed earlier, by using YOU and YOUR in your writing, you very effectively speak to your reader's self interest.

Alright let's go on with step two...

Let your reader know the advantages they receive from your product/service.

Real early in your letter you'll need to tell the reader the advantages they receive from your product/service.

All humans are looking for the answers to three questions when they hear from you:

1) So what?
2) Who cares?
3) What's in it for me?

In other words, your reader is asking you, "What can this product/service do for me?"

You must show your prospect/customer the advantage of using your product/service.

And always remember, it's not what your product/service is that counts, it's only what RESULTS your product/service can provide your reader.

In step number three it's important to provide proof that you can deliver the advantages and results you promise. Probably the easiest way is through testimonials from happy customers.

Testimonials from real people are very powerful.

It plays on the middle brain, the "me too" brain, the "keep up with the Jones" brain, the "herd mentality" brain, the mammalian brain.

This is also called giving "social proof". Which is one of the six great persuaders. (More about the other five some other time.)

The fourth step is to persuade the reader by appealing to their emotional wants, desires, and fears. Before you ask you reader to take action, now is your last chance to talk to the emotions once again by speaking directly to the hopes, fears, wants, and desires of your reader.

And the final step is to get your reader to take action now by making an irresistible offer.

Make them an offer for a free bonus, a special price, a long risk-free guarantee, anything that will build up the value of your offer for your product/service so that your offer is simply to good to pass up. Your offer's value to the reader should be perceived to be much, much greater than the dollars that you're asking of your customer/prospect.

Once you have built up the value sufficiently, then your customer will buy.

Very simply, once you benefit the customer more than the dollars in their pocket, you will have made a sale and gained a new or repeat customer.

Okay, there's the "format"...so how do you fill in the details, you ask?

Here's the easy way to get a great sales letter or ad.

1) Tape record your conversations with your customers and prospects or have someone interview you and answer questions that lead to sales on your product/service.

2) Transcribe the recordings and then highlight each selling point for easy identification.

3) Rank each selling point 1 to 10, 10 being the highest...and have someone else do this too, preferably a customer or someone who is impartial to your product/service. Your results will vary from the opinions of a customer, etc...interesting, isn't it?

4) Now cut up the sheets of paper and divide them into three piles. The first pile has the results that your product/service provides (the benefits), the second pile has interesting facts about your product/service (the features), and the third is just some points that really aren't that focused in showing the advantages of your product/service.

5) Throw away the third group and then rank the other two groups (the benefits and features) from the ranking of 10 down to 1.

6) Now throw away your point that have a ranking of 5 or less...keep only your most powerful points.

7) Okay, now you're ready to start writing, but don't sit down to "write" a sales letter or ad. Just write a personal conversation to a someone you really care about (one of your customers, for example, actually use their name to get you started...Dear Bill:..) and use the 5-step template above to help organize your letter/ad.

Once you've got it written, then read it out loud so you can see where the flow of your letter slows down or where certain phrases make you stumble. If they make you stumble, then be assured your reader will stumble there also. And let someone else read it aloud too.

Edit your letter and be sure to use short sentences, short paragraphs, and speak in everyday language. In other words don't use "insider lingo" that your reader won't understand and don't use language that only a "rocket scientist" or some "PhD" would use, just use common everyday words and talk like a real everyday kind of person.

And be sure to break up your letter with eye-appealing layout and sub-heading to make it easy for the eye to read.

Some "Q and A"...

QUESTION: I've put together my ad and sales letter but I'm just not getting the responses I'd like to see, and it seems like I'm not getting anywhere. Can you give me a few tips on what to do different?

ANSWER: As always, let's start by focusing on the most important person in the world to you, your prospects/customers. The first thing to do is to make sure that you have identified a highly targeted niche of prospects to send your ad to or to drop your ad into their "pond".

Remember that you're trying to reach the right market, with the right message, at the right time. Or as we relate it to fishing...the right pond, with the right bait, when the fish is hungry.

Now first to find the right pond. Look around the website forums and interest groups online, the classified ad areas that have something to do with your product/service, the membership directory and do a search for people with like interests or occupations, any place where your target market gathers to discuss their problems and solutions.

There's your market, your pond, your list.

Now let's talk about your "bait"...your ad and sales letter.

The first thing you should try to change to see if you get better results is your headline. Test at least five different headlines. You don't have the right to tell your market which headline they will best respond to. So don't think that you know which headline is best without testing at least five, one against the other. Let your market tell you which headline is the winner.

It's very inexpensive to test headlines online, so there's no excuse not to test headlines in your ads and letters.

Make sure that you're highlighting the BENEFITS of your product/service (the results your customer receives), rather than the FEATURES (or facts) about your product/service.

People respond (BUY) benefits and results...they say "that's interesting" to features and facts.

Always talk in benefits and results first, instead of features and facts.

Here's a simple sure-fire format to help you get started:

You get...<benefit/result>...from...<feature/fact>.

Give "social proof" (testimonials) that others have gotten the benefits/results that you offer.

Work on your guarantee. Make it longer, make it better-than-money-back, make it lifetime, make it no risk to the buyer to do business with you (by the way, if you can't guarantee and deliver results then you shouldn't be asking for anyone's money).

Work on your call to action. It may be better to give your reader a couple of options. One to order, another to make a phone call to talk and get a little more info before making a decision. This works well and isn't very threatening to your reader. It's no risk to them to give you a call to talk with someone before committing to a purchase. Then you or your staff can explain things and make a real human connection with your prospect.

Test your prices and bonuses too. The will let you know how to build value to your offer (value equals how the results of your offer exceeds the money it costs...always strive to allow your buyer benefit many times more than you will...and tell them so).

Okay, let's look at the timing. Fish are not always hungry, are they?

Your offer has to be presented not only to the right market (pond), with the right offer (benefits/results/offer/guarantee/price/value), but also at the right time in your prospect's life.

This can be tricky and this is where repetition of your offer comes in.

Try followups (at least seven) and make different offers, package different bonuses in with your main offer, ad a twist here and there, try different pricings, etc.

Just know that by asking for your information, the reader has identified themselves as a "fish" or prospect, and it's just a matter of time before they get hungry for your offer...as long as it is appetizing to them.

(go on to next chapter now)

Bonus Chapter 6...

"Ten Hot Tips To Increase Your Sales...Fast"

1. It's The List - always start making your offers to your own customer lists and people who have requested information from you in the past. Then acquire other names by doing your own research from databases, organizations, etc. You can also purchase lists of names from list brokers. Just remember, the more specifically targeted the list, the better response you'll get to your specific offer.

2. Get To Know Your Customers - get on all the mailing lists you can that target your customers (that's right, you'll be on your competitors mailing lists). Study all the offers you see and find the best of each and come up with your own way of making the your offer more attractive to your customer.

3. Your Unique Selling Advantage - come up with the one major benefit that you offer that no one else does and make that the emphasis of your offer. You must be perceived to being unique.

4. Make Sure Your Headline Is Pulling Them In - remember your headline is your ad for your ad and counts for more than 80% or more of your ads success. Test, test, test one headline against another leaving everything else the same. Once you have a headline that pulls by a major percentage greater than the others, let that become the "control" to keep testing against in the future. By the way, the name of your company or your name at the top of your ad (or even letterhead) in not a headline...there is no major benefit for your customer stated.

5. Salesmanship In Print - give full and complete details in you ad (or sales letter too). People will read long ads as long as they are interested in what they read. Ads are never too long, only too boring! Give them benefits, benefits, benefits...advantages, advantages, advantages...not features of your product/service.

6. Use A P.S. - restate your major benefit and give them a reason to act now (special price, time limit, quantity limit, etc.). Use it as a second chance to state your headline when it's time to order.

7. The Layout Of Your Ad - make your ad and all support material attractive to the eye...easy to read. Use different spacing, subheadlines, typestyles, capitalizations, characters, etc. to create excitement and interest.

8. Frequency - don't mail out anything just once and expect a response. Humans are terrific procrastinators, it's what they do best. It takes on the average 7 times before you establish a position in the brain of your prospect...7 times!

9. Always Ask For The Sale - after you've gone through all the trouble of making your complete sales presentation, don't forget to ask for the sale. Tell the reader what they must do NOW to receive the benefits you're offering. Always include ordering instructions (800#, order form, whatever).

10. Go to... SmallBizSuccessCoach.com

I know, I know...a blatant commercial pitch! Remember...always ask for the order! <grin>

Things To Work On

1. Come up with 10 headlines for your product/service that promise your target customer the greatest benefit that you can offer. Test them one against the other until you come up with the obvious winner.

2. Next try to put together a package deal to your offer...some extra freebies, or some extra services that you throw in for free just because they do business with you and no one else. Make it very exclusive to your product/service

Try these two things this month and write me a testimonial letting me know how it changes the results you're getting.

(go on to next chapter now)

126

Bonus Chapter 7...

"The Six Secret Persuaders To Use In Every Offer You Make"

Since everything that you sell is going to be bought by a human being, wouldn't it be great if you knew the six great influencers on human behavior?

When these six secret motivators are included in a sales presentation, whether it be in a short ad, a longer ad, a sales letter, or a long presentation...any offer at all, I've seen amazing results.

I've put these in order of use in the marketing process, sometimes they'll need to overlap or even change the order to fit the situation.

SECRET PERSUADER #1 - What happens in nature when a vacuum is created or found? That's right, there is an attempt to fill that void. Now remember, human nature also follows the laws of nature.

Most all of the time, when someone does a person a favor, does something nice, gives them something of value for free, or basically provides any kind gesture, whether it be large or small, without any apparent "strings attached"...this act provides an imbalance in the relationship...in "nature"...in "human nature".

And there is an incredible amount of subconscious pressure on the recipient to give back in some way. This filling in the void, we call...

"RECIPROCATION"

In marketing the word FREE, has the most response of any word that you could ever use. That's why so many marketers use it over, and over, and over again. Everybody wants something for free, don't you?

You say, "Yes, but is there any obligation?"

And the answer is, of course, "Free, with no cost or obligation."

Now, why does this obligate the person anyway?

Because if something of real value is given to the person, an imbalance is created, a void in nature that will need to be filled. The void may not be filled immediately, but if the recipient has gotten great value and use from the gift, there will always be a nagging subconscious motivation to reciprocate in some manner.

Now let me say this, you'll find that some people just don't seem to reciprocate at all.

Could it be that they didn't receive the full value of your offer, they didn't appreciate the full value of your offer, or are they are just "non-reciprocating" people?

The first two are your problems, because you should always make sure someone knows, understands and appreciates the full value of what they are receiving.

The last one, the "non-reciprocating" person, well, you need to just move on. Some people go through their whole lives never learning how great it is to help others along the way, and being helped along the way by others.

So the first thing to do in your marketing is to make a risk-free offer to your prospect...FREE is always good...with no cost or "obligation" of course.

SECRET PERSUADER #2 - Now what you're trying to accomplish step-by-step-by-step, little-by-little is to develop a relationship with your prospective customer.

And the first thing you would like them to do is to take a small action step and just "raise their hand a little" to let you know they're interested and have them ASK for the FREE offer.

Now I didn't just say give them the FREEBIE without them at least asking for it, did I? No, they need to show some action toward you, sort of like a fish nibbling on the bait, before you spend your money or time giving them the FREEBIE.

This is done by using a short ad and offering a Special FREE Report or giving a FREE sample if they stop by the store, etc.

The idea here is to get an ever-so-small...

"COMMITMENT with CONSISTENCY"

...from the person, because when someone takes action, even if it's very small, they have made a commitment. And most humans (at least the ones you want to do business with) are still raised to honor their commitments...and to be consistent in their behaviors.

Throughout your relationship they will be testing your commitments and consistencies, you will be encouraging their commitment and consistency in buying from you.

A little note here, it's always better to have the boat reel to the fish, rather than have the fish know he's caught and just reeled in and yanked into the boat. In other words, small commitments from your prospect will help them jump in your boat, and have it all be their own idea.

SECRET PERSUADER #3 - Have you ever heard that before someone will buy from you, they must first "know, like and trust" you?

Getting someone to know you is the easiest, you just throw your offer at them and they'll "know" you.

However, the second step is to get them to **"LIKE"** you.

May I suggest that the quickest way to get someone to like you is for you to let them know that you like them (reciprocation at work here?).

Please understand that not all people are going to like you and you're not going to like all people. But if you take this approach you have a lot better odds of finding customers.

And always write your ads and letters as a personal note to a real, live and breathing person. Just use plain talk, like when you talk with your closest friends, and please no "hi-tech psycho-babble" using big 25 cent words that even your mother doesn't know. Keep it simple.

Now this "know you, like you, and trust you" leads us to the next power persuader...

SECRET PERSUADER #4 - I don't know about you, but when I hear ANYBODY say "trust me"...then that's the last thing I'm going to do. When YOU ask someone to trust you, it sends up all kinds of red warning lights, flashing brighter than a five-alarm fire.

So how do you get people to trust you quickly and go ahead and buy from you. You've got to use the secret persuader called...

"SOCIAL PROOF"

This is to simply provide your prospect with testimonials and endorsements of your products/services. There is nothing more powerful than your happy customers telling in their own words (not your cleverly crafted words) why they like doing business with you.

SECRET PERSUADER #5 - To get people to buy from you, you've got to take a leadership role with them. Remember, you've gone through the first four persuaders with them and they're still with you...now's the time to tell them what they should do to take action and buy.

You must be or present yourself as an...

"AUTHORITY"

You need to be the authority figure...the expert...the only person to buy from (who has told them, you?...no...your customers and third parties (by endorsements or other social proof...articles written about you, books, articles, newsletters you've written, etc.)

Interestingly, most be people don't want to make a decision and it's better that you give them a plan of action to say "yes" to. At this stage, people are wanting you to lead them (they already know, like and trust you).

SECRET PERSUADER #6 - There is one persuader that tends to help motivate humans to action and you must create and manage this to your advantage in every offer you make. It is the power persuader called...

"SCARCITY"

People want things that solve their problems or make them feel good about themselves that are of good quality...and they want it even more if the quantity is limited.

Remember the laws of supply and demand.

If the demand for a product/service is high and the supply is low, then the price that kind be charged will be accepted readily (or you may be able to raise your prices to create more profit per unit sold).

Be sure to include all six of these persuaders in all of your offers (ads, sales letter, presentations, etc.). You'll see a dramatic increase in your net results.

My friend, since you're interested, for more background and details on these techniques, I recommend you read "Influence--The Psychology of Persuasion" by Robert Cialdini. I've made it easy for you to order it at a discount at www.amazon.com ...and hurry, supplies are limited.

(by the way, can you count the six persuaders in the preceding paragraph?...they are all there)

You can also read more about Dr. Cialdini's real-life research on how these six principals are used by visiting...

InfluenceAtWork.com

(go on to next chapter now)

Bonus Chapter 8...

"How To Use One Of Six Power Persuaders To Increase Leads And Sales Now"

Have you ever noticed how most people have trouble making decisions on their own?...And a lot of the time they take the "wait and see" approach to their buying habits?

Well, that's just "human nature" for the majority of people.

So how do you combat this "quirk" in human nature?

Here's a very important marketing magic rule...

> **"don't fight human nature, use it as a marketing tool to your advantage."**

Use two techniques of the great persuader...SOCIAL PROOF.

#1 is TESTIMONIALS.

Testimonials work because it gives your reader assurance that someone else has done business with you before and has received full value and the desired results that you promise. In other words, you deliver what they pay for...and more!

It's great to get good testimonials out of the blue from your customers, but you also may need to ask for them from your good customers too.

How?

Send your good customers a short letter letting them know that you are updating your marketing materials and would appreciate a short letter from them describing their delight in having done business with you. Describing your great service, credibility, happiness with desired results, etc...

Now don't go and try to write testimonials for yourself. I don't quite know why it is, but they always sound fake (actually I do know why they sound fake, it's because they are fake).

You know you can spot a fake testimonial and so can I...and your prospective customers can too.

And here's an even more powerful persuader.

#2 is ENDORSEMENTS.

Now I don't mean the type of endorsements that you see on TV by some highly paid "celeb" spokesperson.

No, just a real life person who describes their experience with you and your product/service in a way that's very believable, in a person to person manner.

It helps if they have some "center of influence" reputation but it's not totally necessary for the endorsement to work well.

The reason that these two persuading techniques work is that people always make decisions on an emotional level first and them justify that decision with logic.

So by using testimonials and endorsements you help people buy:

* emotionally (making them comfortable) and

* logically (someone else has received the desired results)

Use these techniques of SOCIAL PROOF, they work.

(go on to next chapter now)

Bonus Chapter 9...

"The Most Important Part of Your Ad...and Why!"

Is there a most important part of your sales message?

Absolutely.

Why is it more important than the other parts?

80%+ of the effectiveness of your ad depends on it...and if it's good, it can increase your response up to 1700%.

Why does a good one get these kinds of results?

Like everything in effective marketing that you've learned here, it's all tied to human psychology and emotions.

What is this one thing that can be so hard to come up with, yet so very easy to find an effective one?

It's your headline.

Direct marketing studies have tested and shown that 80%+ of the success of your ad is the drawing power of your headline. And by testing headlines, one against another with the same sales offer included, a good one can increase your ad's response up to 1700%!!!!

That leads to a seemingly simple question..."why?"

See if what I'm saying makes sense to you.

At the subconscious level, each and every human is wanting to self-improve (move toward feeling good) or interested in solving a problem (avoiding pain).

By the way, avoiding pain is a much greater human motivator than self-improvement. Just look how fast someone wants to take action when they are having a major problem or are in great emotional, physical, or financial pain.

And interestingly, self-improvement is many times full of emotional, physical, and financial pain, isn't it?

You're trying new things to expand and many times there are stumbling blocks along the way that can be difficult to overcome...you see, actually positive growth can be painful.

So many times the human spirit will give up because they are experiencing pain...when they were promised feeling better!...emotionally, physically, financially, etc.

Now you can understand why it's hard to get someone to try something new, even if it's positive and good for them.

They are currently in their "comfort zone", not feeling any pain, and you try to get them to move ahead and "risk" feeling new pains that they haven't dealt with yet...with the hope of doing better, and not feeling these new pains in the future.

The result...they do nothing.

Now sit back for a moment and think about what you're feeling.

I've just described your frustration and pain as a marketer.

You've made an offer to someone, an offer you believe to be of great value and importance.

Unfortunately for you, your prospect didn't take notice or respond at all.

Why?

One of two things.

They were either in their "comfort zone" and did not currently have the pain you described, or...the good feelings that you offered were not "perceived by them" (their only reality) to be worth the emotional, financial, physical and time cost (risk/pain) they may endure to achieve the end result...so they do nothing.

Ouch, you feel your pain and frustration.

Okay, here's where your headline comes in (finally, you say, he's getting to the point).

Your headline has the ability to break through to the lower levels of the emotional brain of your human prospect. As you've heard me say time and time again, all humans (you and I included) make all decisions on an emotional basis first, and then justify that decisions to ourselves and others with "logic".

Therefore, your headline must appeal to the emotional brain, not the the "logical" brain.

Your headline must provoke curiosity in your reader by bringing up a problem (pain) they are having, or by promising a great new benefit or solution to their problem...or here's the best kept marketing secret...BOTH!!!

Always try for both...but as always...test, test, test.

So here's what you do...

Start analyzing all the ads and newspaper/magazine articles (they have headlines, don't they?) you read and figure out whether they are offering pain avoidance or new comforts, or both. See how the headline draws you in with the benefits of reading more.

(go on to next chapter now)

Bonus Chapter 10...

"Seven Secrets To Getting More Responses To Your Ads"

 # 1 - As hard as you try to come up with a product or service that offers benefits and advantages over and beyond your competition, and no matter how much time and talent your pour into crafting a great ad, sales letter and website, the most important success secret in marketing is...

"THE LIST"

In other words, the people you're going to send your ad and/or sales letter to.

The hottest list you'll ever have is the list of customers that have already bought from you...too many marketers overlook this simple fact. Your customers have already made the relationship decisions of getting to know you, like you, and trust you. Enough to buy from you in the past. And if you've done well for them, there is the highest likelihood they will buy in the future.

Make sure you keep in close contact with them and give them special deals, offers, incentives to do more and more business with you.

The next hottest list are people who have bought what you are selling or something similar from someone else. In other words, you have to find other companies/people who already have a good relationship with your future customers. You may be able to purchase their list or at least work a deal to run an ad to their list for a flat fee or a percentage of the profits.

Listen, it's taken that company/person most likely many years and years, and many thousands upon thousands of dollars to attract that customer to them and to develop the great relationship they have. And usually, for pennies on the dollar of what it cost them to acquire the customer, you can work a deal to have access to a very hot list of prospects that would make very good customers for you too.

Always remember, marketing is a lot like fishing...you've got to get to the right pond, when the fish are hungry, with the bait they want.

What you're looking for is someone who has already "stocked" the pond!

Just begin to think who already has access to the prospective customers you are looking for.

 # 2 - As we've discussed before, humans make all decisions first with their emotions and then justify that decision with logic. So doesn't it make sense that you should market your way into their brain with what are called...

"EMOTIONAL HOTBUTTONS"

You've got to find out and present to your customer/prospect the benefits and advantages they are looking for in the products and services you offer.

This can't just be a list of the features of your product or service. No...you must specifically tell and show your customer/prospect the "END RESULTS" they will have when they purchase your product/service. In other words, tell and show them how they will BENEFIT from the purchase from you.

Never again just tell someone the features. Always talk of the benefits that your customer/prospect gets first, and then tell them the feature of the product that provides it.

Such as...

You'll catch your limit of trophy bass five times faster, with your new natural-action and natural-color fishing lure that bass just can't resist.

 # 3 - It's been shown through repeated testing over the last 100 years by the top marketers that AT LEAST 80% of the success of your ad/salesletter/website is your...

"HEADLINE"

This is what grabs your readers attention and draws them into your ad/letter/website.

It must be based on BENEFITS that are immediately recognized as desirable by your target market. It must make a big promise to solve a problem or make them feel good, or both. In other words, to provide pleasure (gain) or avoid pain (loss)...or both. These are the emotions that drive the human being to action the fastest.

The only way your going to find the best headline is to test, test, test one against another until you find one that outpulls by a WIDE percentage and then you'll use that one as your "control" and come up with others to test against it to see just "how high is high" as far as your results go.

 # 4 - Once you've gotten their attention and shown them why they should care and what's in it for them, it's time to make them...

"YOUR OFFER AND GUARANTEE"

Your offer should be very simple and specific.

You get this benefit, that benefit, this result and that result and with your complete satisfaction guaranteed, or this or that will happen (i.e. refund, extra this or that, etc.).

And you must build up the value of your offer by framing it in comparison to what others are charging or doing...and how you are offering much, much more for less or the same price.

 # 5 - Now if you want to increase the response to your offers, you must add something extra to your offers, something maybe a little be different than your main offer known as...

"FREE BONUSES"

Free Bonuses can offer other benefits that are different from your main product/service, but the interesting thing is that many times people will buy because of the bonus offered. Yes, they are interested in the main product/service, but the free bonus is the thing they just couldn't pass up.

It doesn't have to cost you much or cost you anything.

You ask, "Anything?...You mean nothing?"

That's right. Many times you'll be able to find other business owners who would be very willing to allow you to offer something of theirs as a free bonus in your main offer. I've done this lot's of times, on both sides of the deal.

Sometimes I ask someone to use their special report as a free bonus for an offer I'm making and other times, I make something I've written a free bonus for someone else's offer. It works great...try it sometime.

 # 6 - It's a fact, most people just don't have much self-motivation, so your job as a marketer is to make things very easy for your reader. Once you've presented your reader with all the reasons why they want to do something by showing the benefits and results they'll have, you have to provide them...

"EASY ORDERING OF THE PRODUCT/SERVICE or AN EASY WAY TO ASK FOR MORE INFORMATION"

Make your order instructions crystal clear, whether it be to purchase or to receive more info from you.

 # 7 - Here's where most marketers just plain "drop the ball". After you've gotten the customer to buy or the prospect to ask for more information, you've got to...

"FOLLOWUP"

Your big profits are in the continuing relationship that you are building with each and every one of your customers and soon to be customers. To much money slips right through the hands of marketers all over the world because of this simple truth. You must persistently followup and continue to build on the relationship you've started. It's cost you time and money to find the customer, now it's time to cultivate like a farmer and finally harvest from the relationship.

I've used the word "relationship" here a lot in this chapter. You've got to "love your customers" and put them first in your mind, because the greatest asset you can ever have as a business owner is not your equipment, not your employees, not anything else...the most important asset that any business has is its...

"CUSTOMERS"

And it's kind of funny that I've never seen "Customers" as an asset listed on any company's balance sheet.

(go on to next chapter now)

Bonus Chapter 11...

"How To Instantly Get Your Prospect's Attention -- And Give Them The Reason Why They Should Do Business With You Instead Of Anyone Else (Or How To Design Your USA)"

You know we keep hammering the idea that your headline is going to account for 80%+ of the success of your ads. Well here's something that will help you come up with headlines and to use it in all your marketing -- webpages, salesletters, headlines, banners, you name it.

It's your Unique Selling Advantage -- or USA for short.

Your USA states very quickly the problem your prospect is having, how bad the problem is, that you provide results-oriented solutions and that you are the best source for the solution to their problem, and that you like to get referrals too.

Most people when asked what exactly do you do, don't have a good answer for it. They just respond with, "well, I'm in the <fill-in-the-blank> business" or "We sell widgets".

This is not good.

No, you need to be able to very quickly give the person an understanding of what you offer to someone who needs your product or service, whether it be themselves or someone they know.

The goal is to get them to ask you, "how do you do that?" or "what is it?" after you tell them your USA.

That opens the door for your complete sales presentation, where you can describe all the benefits and advantages that someone gets by doing business with you.

Here's an example for accounting services -- before and after...

Before: We do tax returns.

After:

Do you know how much it hurts to work all year long to make a living only to realize that you worked until May just to pay your income taxes -- What we do is review the tax laws inside and out to find every legal way of reducing your taxes so you get to keep as much as possible and build your net worth...fast. Who do you know who would be interested in that?

See the difference?

The "before" just gave the typically answer to the question -- the "after" gave the reason why someone should do business with you -- to benefit them or someone they know.

Here's another one...

Before: I help people with their marketing.

After:

Businesses of all kinds have one common problem, how to get more business profit to their bottom line -- what I do is design marketing systems that generate guaranteed sales results (not empty expensive promises) that leverage your marketing dollar 5 to 10 to 20 or more times to bring more bottom line profits for the same (or less) advertising dollar -- guaranteed. Who do you know who'd be interested in that?

Do you see how you can use this simple "formula" for your business or offer of any kind?

The formula is this...

Do you know <describe the problem>...<then make the problem worse>...What we do is <state your approach to achieve the major result, benefit, and solution to their problem>...Who do you know who'd be interested in that?

Give it a try -- come up with a few versions and test them over the next month to see which one comes out the "winner" for you.

(go on to next chapter now)

Bonus Chapter 12...

"How To Increase Your Sales And Responses To Your Ads -- Now!"

I had a call this week from a client that was having cashflow problems. She was having to juggle things around a little so she could keep her suppliers paid (can anyone relate to that?).

After talking for a while, I said "I think we're trying to fix the wrong end of the problem. You just need more cash coming in the FRONT door -- that will take care of the bills to be paid."

Now I confess, that's not rocket science -- but sometimes we get thinking in one direction and we get blinded to the solutions.

So what did she need to do? I asked her a few questions...

1. Who makes the best customer for you? I mean exactly who are they -- write down their name(s).

2. What makes them a good customer? They buy a lot, they pay on time, they refer others to you, they're nice people, they're repeat customers, etc...

3. Wouldn't it be GREAT if you had a whole bunch more customers just like that one (or them)?

YES -- YES -- YESSSSSSSS !!!!

Do you think that would help solve cashflow problems?

YES -- YES -- YESSSSSSSSS !!!!

Right you are.

Here's what you do...

Get out some paper and your "thinking cap" -- you're about to discover how to make your business up to 5 times (or more) profitable.

1. Admit to yourself that you're probably making 80% of your sales from 20% of your customers (yes, the old 80-20 rule at work again).

2. You're spending most of your time trying to get the 80% of your customers to be like the upper 20% -- I've got some news for you...

"IT AIN'T GONNA HAPPEN!"

3. You've got to write down SPECIFICALLY the traits of your best customers and then get more people like them.

Let's stop here and remember the comparison to fishing. Well, if you're going after trophy bass, and you keep catching catfish, then you're doing something wrong (the bass are your 20% good customers and the catfish are your 80%).

Go fishing for the 20% good ones by knowing everything about them and giving THEM want they WANT.

4. Sit down and take the time and effort to write down everything about your good customers and what they want -- and target all of your marketing toward those top customers.

5. Ask your best customers to help you locate more people like themselves through a referral system you set in place -- you'll find many of them will be happy to help you -- you've helped them and they like to reciprocate.

Now here's something interesting, what would your business be like if all your customers were like the top 20% of the top 20% of your customer base -- that means the top 4% of all your customers.

Do you think your business might just surpass your wildest dreams?

YES -- YES -- YESSSSSSS !!!!!

Get busy and analyze your customer base -- spend 80% of your time working with the top 20% (or top 4%) of your customers -- and attract more people like them by knowing everything you possible can about them and then crafting your marketing toward that market (person, pond, fish, etc)

(go on to next chapter now)

Bonus Chapter 13...

"The Little Secret That The World's Sharpest Marketers Use To Increase Their Results Up To 1000% or More"

You've heard it from me time and time again, the three most important words in marketing are...

Test -- Test -- Test

You test one headline against another, one offer against another, one guarantee against another, one price against another -- you test each variable of your ad to find the combination that will get you the best results for the dollar you invest in marketing.

This alone will help boost the results you get from your marketing efforts and will turn effort into dollars at your bottom line.

Now that's where most marketers stop -- once they find something that's working pretty good they just stop short of hitting the "mother lode".

Here's the next step -- the secret that the world's sharpest marketers use to leverage their marketing up to 1000% or more.

There's three more words that come into play now, three words that leverage your testing. The three words are...

Diversify -- Diversify -- Diversify

The idea is to take your tested ad and now present it in a variety of ways so that your customers have multiple ways of getting your message and responding to you. This tends to have a synergistic effect on your market -- kind of piling on the message from every direction.

Let's say that you've used ads to test your headline, your offer, your price, your guarantee, your free bonuses, and the overall format of your ad and sales letter, and they are getting very good results.

Now take the same tested ad and sales letter, and begin to use it in your website. And then use it on postcards, either leading to a recorded voice message, call in response, write in response to get more info from your sales letter or from a person answering questions.

Use the same ad in a telemarketing campaign, newspaper ads, radio, TV ads on cable, on your business cards, flyers, newspaper inserts, you name it, just begin leveraging the successful work you've done finding out what your market responds to by beginning to use new ways for your market to hear about and respond to your offer.

This is how you're going to be able to recoup the time, effort and money if took to test your initial offer and turn it into a goldmine of profits for you.

Now, will all of these new avenues to you be all home-runs -- no, some will do better than others. Just keep testing each as you go, and tweak them a little, and leverage your marketing to bring in more leads, more sales, more customers, and more back-end sales than you can have imagined.

Start today thinking about all the ways you can now leverage the successful ads/letters/offers you've developed through your testing -- never stop trying to find out how high is high -- keep reaching higher and higher and the results will amaze you.

www.ingramcontent.com/pod-product-compliance
Lightning Source LLC
Chambersburg PA
CBHW051527170526
45165CB00002B/635